JERSEY BREAKS

ALSO BY ROBERT PINSKY

ROBERT PINSKY

JERSEY BREAKS

BECOMING
AN
AMERICAN POET

W. W. NORTON & COMPANY
Independent Publishers Since 1923

Copyright © 2022 by Robert Pinsky

For information about permission to reproduce
selections from this book, write to Permissions,
W. W. Norton & Company, Inc.,
500 Fifth Avenue, New York, NY 10110

For information about special discounts for bulk purchases,
please contact W. W. Norton Special Sales at
specialsales@wwnorton.com or 800-233-4830

Manufacturing by Lake Book Manufacturing
Book design by Brooke Koven
Production manager: Anna Oler

ISBN 978-0-393-88204-9

W. W. Norton & Company, Inc.
500 Fifth Avenue, New York, N.Y. 10110
www.wwnorton.com

W. W. Norton & Company Ltd.
15 Carlisle Street, London W1D 3BS

1 2 3 4 5 6 7 8 9 0

To Jill Kneerim

Gimme a break.

—FOLK SAYING

❧

Sorrow would break the seal stamped over time
And set the baskets where the bough is bent.

—LOUISE BOGAN,
"Simple Autumnal"

❧

But Love has pitched his mansion in
The place of excrement;
For nothing can be sole or whole
That has not been rent.

—WILLIAM BUTLER YEATS,
"Crazy Jane Talks with the Bishop"

CONTENTS

PROLOGUE

GIVEN MY BACKGROUND, a friend asked me, how is it I became a poet rather than a criminal or an optometrist?

I could quibble. My father Milford Pinsky was an optician, not an optometrist. (A common mistake.) And it's true that his father Dave Pinsky was a criminal. But as my aunt Thelma used to say, her pop was in the liquor business, and it happened to be during Prohibition. That was the era when Dave, my Zaydee Pop, as I called him, pursued the liquor business in our hometown, Long Branch, New Jersey.

Trivial and significant, stupid and profound, like a family oppressive and nurturing, like the larger world seductive and treacherous: My feelings about the town are as confused as can be. My bedeviled patriotism, my need for the lofty outcast art of poetry, my C-student's distrust of worldly rewards and punishments, the inward voice that spurs me to bring together disparate times, places and things, that attraction to a mishmosh. All began in Long Branch.

If I have a story to tell, it's how the failures and aspirations of a certain time and place led to poetry.

JERSEY BREAKS

1

A Provincial Sense of Time

A T A Library of Congress luncheon in Washington in the year 2000 the speakers included Congressman Frank Pallone of Long Branch, New Jersey. Frank Pallone's family and mine had known one another for three generations. His father, Frank Pallone, Sr., was a respected cop of the old-school kind who might catch a thirteen-year-old shoplifting and lock the kid into a cell for a few hours, then let him go with a lecture. The congressman's mother was a figure in Long Branch town legend. She went to the beach looking great in her leopard-spotted, two-piece bathing suit, with her two little boys, Frank and his brother, togged out in their matching leopard-spotted trunks.

Frank Pallone has said that to understand my poetry you need to understand our town. I know what he means. The races and ethnicities, with all the other blends, resistances, suspicions, borrowings, intermarriages, rivalries and molten alloys of American cuisine, art and social life, all concentrated in a seashore resort that was near great cities yet, by definition, *away* from them: that was a world the congressman and I had known all our lives.

Also at the head table that day was another person I admired. The elegant Lyn Chase had just arrived on a flight from New York to attend this Washington event in her capacity as president of the Academy of American Poets. A beautiful woman in her seventies, Lyn was a sharp-witted patron of the arts, charming and very rich and accustomed to getting her way.

"I got off the plane and realized I had no credit cards or money," she said when I greeted her. "So I had to pick up a man who would give me a ride to get here."

After Representative Pallone finished his remarks at the microphone, Lyn Chase asked, "Is the congressman coming back?"

"No, he headed back to the Hill."

"Good," I was surprised to hear her say. "I hate his brother."

I thought of the two little boys in their leopard swimsuits, and also of the recent mayoral campaign in Long Branch. Adam Schneider had been reelected mayor, but Frank Pallone's younger brother John, unexpectedly, challenged Adam, running a failed campaign against him. The election campaign had gotten a bit rough, as I heard from my aunts and cousins, straining a long friendship between the two families, the Schneiders and the Pallones. There were lots of people in town with those names—exactly the kind of thing the congressman remarked on in my poems. Over dessert and coffee I tried to explain this Long Branch story at some length—maybe I even mentioned Marian Pallone's bathing suit—while the Library of Congress officials at our table and Lyn Chase listened politely. As I finished talking a little too much, I said how surprised I was that Lyn knew about the congressman's family. How had she come to hate his brother? She responded mildly:

"What I said was, 'I ate his butter.'"

*   *   *

I SOMETIMES think with my ears and voice, putting music above meaning. It's a habit that has been my failing and my calling.

Little Silver, Hazlet, Perth Amboy, Rahway and Secaucus were stops on the New York and Long Branch Railroad. I don't know much about those places. But the consonants and vowels of their names, chanted by old-school conductors on the way to Penn Station, made a familiar, seductive music. My many aunts and uncles lived in Hoboken, Hackensack, Summit, Passaic, Hopewell and The Oranges. Which family lived where I don't remember, but those place names made a verbal harmony like what I found years later in sixteenth century lyrics by John Dowland and Thomas Campion.

MY MIS-HEARING "I ate his butter" is an example of the provincial sense of time. In a proper understanding of time, you focus on causes and effects over centuries or years or hours. But from a limited, intensely local viewpoint the centuries and years and hours might be understood through a particular place and its people. That's how I mis-heard Lyn Chase's plain sentence. Space, in the form of a town and its imagination, preempted the reality of time.

In a certain kind of place, everything can feel simultaneous. Somewhere in my imagination, along with a rational sense of history, general and personal, I dwell in a cloudy Olden Days where the two little boys with their pretty mother, all three in leopard-spotted swimsuits, walked to the beach down a stairway from the bluff being painted by Winslow Homer, crossing the Boardwalk and Ocean Avenue, where they could buy lunch at Max's Famous Hot Dogs and admire the fast horses of President Grant, who defeated the forces of evil in the Civil War, Grant a friend of Mark Twain and a hard-drinking man who might buy his prohibited whiskey from my Zaydee Pop, or maybe drink it at his Broadway

Tavern, near the Garfield-Grant Hotel—landmarks in an irrational but significant past, that may even include the Dawson's Landing of Mark Twain along with the Dublin of James Joyce: the terrain, as Congressman Frank Pallone recognized, of my imagination.

The blending of different periods in time weaves into the haphazard blending of cultures, in a way the congressman understood. I inherited an edgy mix of hierarchies and goofs, tribal alliances and conflicts, ways of surviving and ways of storytelling, local and global. I grew up inculcated with awe of the past—an awe that was beyond any actual, reliable knowledge of the past.

A personal landmark for me, one of the main junkyards in Long Branch, used to belong to a man named—as if by Charles Dickens—Ash. I went to Izzy Ash's junkyard in the summer of 1962 to buy a used fuel pump for a 1953 Dodge Coronet convertible I would drive to Palo Alto, California. I was going to graduate school at Stanford. Mr. Ash took in that information as he grunted and tugged at a long-handled wrench, to loosen the part I needed from a wrecked Coronet. I told Mr. Ash that I was going to graduate school, not that I was going to be a writer or a poet. As it happens, he knew more than you might expect about going to graduate school. And I had already been embarrassed, earlier that summer, by local people knowing I was, or meant to become, a writer.

A Long Branch boy called Danny Pingitore was having a little success under another name as a television actor. The absurdity of the ambition I was carrying west with me seemed clear when Danny phoned me. I didn't really know him, he was at least five years older than I was, but I knew his brother Anthony. Their mother had run into mine in a store when Danny was in Long Branch for part of July, so he had my phone number.

"Robert, this is Danny Pingitore. Your mother says you are

going out to California to be a writer, and there's something I really need to tell you. Don't go."

"What?"

"Don't go, Robert, I mean it. I know a lot of writers in L.A. They say this is the worst year ever. Nobody is doing hour-long shows anymore. It's all half-hour. Most of the writers already out there can't find work."

So I just told Mr. Ash I was going to Stanford, to graduate school.

In Izzy Ash's class at Long Branch High School there were two outstanding students, both from Jewish families. Both went to Harvard. Mike Abrams and Barry Green were two brilliant and ambitious Long Branch boys whose stories still meant something to Mr. Ash as he braced his feet against the sandy, shadeless, oil-stained dirt of his junkyard and pulled free the fuel pump for my Coronet. He had his generation's respect for what performing well in school could do for somebody whose family had no money or power. So he told me about Mike and Barry.

Mike Abrams went from Harvard College to graduate school and became a distinguished professor, the author of a famous book (*The Mirror and the Lamp*, a study of two Romantic images for poetry; although I had not exactly read the book, I had it on good authority that it was—as it did prove to be—very good). The other Harvard boy in that same high school class, Barry Green, went on to become a rich lawyer, but sadly—as Mr. Ash told me the story he knew I knew—things took a bad turn for Barry Green.

In the course of his climb to success Barry got in deep with the Mob, including a deal that involved selling orange peels to the government for the production of synthetic sugar.

Like those leopard-spotted bathing suits of the Pallone boys and their beautiful mom, the orange peels were a familiar, legendary detail. The words "synthetic sugar" added the authority of specificity to our local tale of a deal saturated in fraud, bribery, chicanery—even, when you think about it, despoiling the United States Treasury in wartime. The dukes and generals of the Mob, protecting the myth of their patriotism, declared that Barry Green would have to go to prison, and so he did. The unthinkable alternative was agreeing to testify, with the likelihood of sudden disappearance. Barry's wife and his two daughters—attractive girls who took elocution lessons, the younger one the first girl in town to play Little League baseball—were taken care of by the dukes and generals.

Meanwhile, the story concluded, Mike Abrams continued the beautiful life of an honored professor at Cornell University, an Ivy League college in a class with Harvard itself, as Mr. Ash said, sighing emphatically. He knew from his daughter Phyllis, my classmate, that I had not been a good student in high school. Retelling the legend of Mike and Barry was his way of indicating respect for my apparent new seriousness. Wiping his head with his forearm, he finished with a moral, expressed by an example from our shared provincial landscape:

"Yes, Robert, there's two different paths in life. It's just like North Broadway and South Broadway."

Broadway's two forks, North and South, form a Y just a couple of blocks from Long Branch's beachfront boardwalk. I nodded solemnly at Mr. Ash's moral, his allegory of those two streets as two paths in life. At the same time, I was thinking that the two paths were pretty much identical. Mr. Ash and I both knew quite well that North Broadway and South Broadway, not notably different from one another, extend to arrive, one long block apart, at exactly the same place, the Atlantic Ocean.

Maybe the point of his story was the reality of shared knowledge—that he and I and the other people in our community all knew the same streets and the same stories. Maybe Mr. Ash was thinking about my probably outliving him, and about my passage into a future as large and mysterious as the ocean itself. California, books, poetry. He wanted to speak as the voice of the past, addressing the future.

II

Rockwell

I N 1947, when I was seven years old and my sister was two, my father got fired from the only job he'd had since he was in high school.

He and my mother were already painfully aware that many of their friends had bought suburban houses in Elberon or Oakhurst, while we were still crowding the four of us into a two-bedroom apartment at 36 Rockwell Avenue, near the corner of Monmouth Avenue. The people who lived on Monmouth, nearly all of them, were Black. One exception was the apartment of my friends Jerry and Irwin Faber, halfway down Monmouth, next door to their father's junkyard, I. Faber Scrap Metal. Irwin was a year younger than me, Jerry a year older. A couple of my exact contemporaries at school, Billy Hanford and Lloyd Weaver, lived near the Fabers, I think one of them next door.

Rockwell was all white people, mostly Italian and Jewish. The racial border with its unspoken rules seemed so unquestioned that I don't think "white flight" was much of an issue, or not yet. It was a poor neighborhood and a segregated one, or you could call it two adjoining poor neighborhoods. In the summer, during the racing season at Monmouth Park, some trainers and exercise boys rented rooms on Rockwell, so for a few weeks it felt more prosperous.

The houses on Monmouth and Rockwell were converted multi-families, originally built as one-family places I can identify now as in the Craftsman style of the 1920s. When I read about the Craftsman style decades later, I remembered how in our apartment the plaster walls were not smooth but crinkly in a random pattern. The irregular-shaped slates of the front walk were in the style of the same period, called crazy-paving. Our walls and our front walk were inspired, at many removes, by the political and social writings of John Ruskin and William Morris, their progressive ideas about art in the lives of ordinary people in the new industrial age of machine-made artifacts.

On the corner of Rockwell and Monmouth, across the street from us, was the office of Julius McKelvie, M.D., the neighborhood's Black doctor. About the same time as I learned about Craftsman houses and William Morris, I discovered that Dr. McKelvie, from his borderland house and office on the corner, was active in the early years of the NAACP. He worked patiently—for years, fruitlessly—to integrate the Long Branch beaches. Only one beach allowed Black people access to the segregated Atlantic Ocean. I remember glimpses from across the street of Dr. McKelvie in his three-piece suit.

At the other end of Monmouth at the corner of Liberty Street was the Tally-Ho Tavern where once in a legendary bar fight somebody bit off a policeman's finger. Next door to the Tally-Ho on Liberty Street a couple of my white friends, Andy Cullen and Martin Gates, lived with their mothers, who may have been sisters. Andy was blond and sweet-natured. Martin was dark-haired, also a good friend but not as open. Andy's father, he confided, was a soldier who died in an explosion when he was guarding an ammunition storehouse. Martin's stepfather was a Comanche Indian, a gloomy man I glimpsed once or twice where he was brooding in a shadowy bedroom. He once had studied to be a dentist, Martin told me.

When I visited Long Branch High School as a smiling sixty-year-old public man, the words I could say that most impressed the assembled students were "Rockwell Avenue." A rough hood to them. A slum, as my mother called it in arguments that intensified after my father lost his job.

Together, partly as a way to deny what seemed his failure in those years, Milford and Sylvia Pinsky took pride in their wit, their skill as dancers and at games, their good looks and their style. Politicians talk about "family values." The Pinsky family valued our belief that we were better-looking than other people. Also funnier. And, with scant justification, that we had better taste, especially in clothes. Henry David Thoreau's dictum "Beware of all enterprises that require new clothes" always makes me think, "That's not how I was brought up." Wardrobe ranked above rehearsal. Sylvia dressed me, her firstborn, carefully. "I washed his white shoelaces," she used to say.

Clothes in a way compensated for real estate. Ads for "ranch-style" tract houses in Elberon that we could not afford celebrated "picture windows" in the living room: wide, factory-sealed panes of glass uninterrupted by movable sash. My mother mocked the "pictures" you could see from the windows of those identical houses. Mainly, the view was the house across the street. Some picture, some ranch!

"Or maybe," she said, "it's all about the picture you can look at when you drive by—Ruthie Edelstein's ass, wide like the window."

After my brother was born, there were three of us kids in the two-bedroom Rockwell Avenue apartment. Sylvia and Milford began searching more desperately for a postwar tract house that might be in their price range. Around that time, at the age of ten or eleven, I began to understand that our family's preening scorn was defensive. Also, in another sense, offensive. The outlaw swagger of my grandfather Dave Pinsky, the barkeeper and former bootlegger, may have inspired that spurious glamour.

I don't know how much my parents' pose of superiority to suburban homeowners was related in my mind later, as a newly literary college kid, to the superiority of James Joyce, Virginia Woolf and Marcel Proust to Pearl Buck and her Nobel Prize or Herman Wouk and the movies based on his best sellers. I was overeager to embrace kinds of judgment I had not done the work to earn. It would be many years before I could absorb the truth—harsh but liberating—that judgment in art depends on work, not hearsay. And it is never final. Willa Cather in *The Song of the Lark* tells the great truth about the serious artist, who dies never being sure of their art's measure. When Cather celebrates the shards of clay vessels that once carried water for the makers who shaped them, fired them and painted them, she conveys how the work itself is the reward and the punishment.

My freshman-year posing did not mean I was stupid, or a phony. I was callow, but I did know how to read with attention. I could recognize the Dublin of Joyce's *Ulysses*, with its bar-talkers and local histories, the provincial web of backbiting, loyalty and gossip. It was like Long Branch, and yet all of that soiled vitality Joyce created was also his reenactment of the *Odyssey*! The good singing voice and sharp tongue of Stephen's father Simon Dedalus and the magnetism of sexy Molly Bloom—performative local figures Dublin at large admired, yet frowned at—stirred recognition in me. Characters respected for their gifts, but not entirely respectable, were a type I recognized. Even the wandering, inventive hero of the *Odyssey* was a bit of a bullshit artist.

In a way, it was music that brought me to *Ulysses*. In my

freshman year at Rutgers, the first-year course Introduction to Literature was required for two kinds of student: prospective majors in English and in physical education. Sections of the course were reserved for one category or the other. Because band rehearsals affected my schedule, I was assigned to a section where everybody else was planning to major in Physical Education. Their commitments to athletic practices and games corresponded to my rehearsal and practice times.

I was in the jazz band, but more practically in the marching band, which released me from carrying a rifle in the Reserve Officers Training Corps. ROTC was required, back then, for the first two years at all American state universities. We were cannon fodder, or at least drill fodder, with our presence giving the real, four-year ROTC students lots of people in uniforms to receive their orders. While other freshmen carried rifles and learned the manual of arms, I carried my Buescher Aristocrat tenor saxophone. And while the others in my Intro to Lit class played sports, I played my part in the lower ranks of the reed section for big-band arrangements of "The Bartlesville Boogie" or "In the Mood."

I don't mean to stereotype the athletes. Some of them were impressive writers and readers. But in that class I shone, and I knew it. Worse, I was pretentious enough and naïve enough to show that I knew it. The teacher, Maurice Charney, gave me extra assignments such as, for example, writing a parody of T. S. Eliot's "The Waste Land" in the style of Raymond Chandler. To take me gently down a notch, and maybe to amuse himself, Charney one day asked me, with a straight face, had I ever read *Ulysses* by James Joyce? Um, I don't think so, sir.

I had never heard of the author or the book, but I got a copy from the library. A lot of it confused me. On the first page, one character emerges from something called the "stairhead" to join others on a tower, where somebody leans on a "gunrest"—maybe they were soldiers at war? Somebody who talks a lot in those first pages is wearing something called a "dressing gown" while holding a "shaving bowl." Those mysterious objects, like Joyce's cloud of literary references, bewildered me in an exciting way. But I loved *Ulysses* as a book about New Jersey. Years later I recognized that feeling when I read an interview with Gabriel García Márquez, where he says that the best South American novel ever written is *The Hamlet* by William Faulkner.

As an ambitious, pseudo-intellectual freshman I set out to understand what Joyce's autobiographical character Stephen Dedalus means by saying that history is "a nightmare from which I am trying to awake." Those words of Joyce's priggish, arrogant young alter ego became a guide for me. In the personal canon that I began to improvise, Elizabeth Bishop, Isaac Babel, William Shakespeare, Ralph Ellison, Emily Dickinson, Franz Kafka, Alan Dugan, Sophocles and Mark Harris dealt with history as a nightmare and the struggle to wake up from it.

With something like religious ardor, I started trying to understand how the young Irish character's declaration about trying to awake might apply to my experience of the United States of America. Working at it, I stumbled into a sort of patriotic American response to Joyce's two-pronged, haughty and blasphemous way of retelling the greatest adventure in Western art. The *Odyssey* gets retold as one day when a lower-class Jew and an ambitious, nightmare-driven young writer bustle and wander around the streets of Dublin.

In my heart of a newly minted highbrow, I adored the story of Stephen Dedalus and Leopold Bloom and their shared journey in history and (maybe) out of it. I recognized the journey the way I recognized Dublin.

Closer to home, I read the poetry of William Carlos Williams, brimming with the mixed and mixed-up immigrant cultures of his New Jersey. I understood why he made his tangled family history defy understanding, in a tribute to his grandmother, "Dedication for a Plot of Ground." I knew at once how the incomprehensibility is the point:

> This plot of ground
> facing the waters of this inlet
> is dedicated to the living presence of
> Emily Dickinson Wellcome
> who was born in England; married;
> lost her husband and with
> her five year old son
> sailed for New York in a two-master;
> was driven to the Azores;
> ran adrift on Fire Island shoal,
> met her second husband
> in a Brooklyn boarding house,
> went with him to Puerto Rico
> bore three more children, lost
> her second husband, lived hard
> for eight years in St. Thomas,
> Puerto Rico, San Domingo, followed
> the eldest son to New York,
> lost her daughter, lost her "baby,"
> seized the two boys of
> the oldest son by the second marriage
> mothered them—they being
> motherless—fought for them
> against the other grandmother
> and the aunts . . .

This poem's disorderly narrative of disorder, with its broken families, forced emigrations and contentious relatives, was exactly the kind of jumbled story I had heard in the conversation of my aunts and uncles—and, even more of a mishmosh, the stories of my great-aunts and great-uncles. In a different way from the Irish exile Joyce, the New Jersey poet Williams, with his Spanish middle name and his English grandmother, made me feel what I still believe is the central issue of American life: the quest for a democratic culture. Were those two words a contradiction in terms? And if not, what might they mean?

Not that I can answer. But overriding every mere election and underlying every national abomination or achievement, I feel the tremendous, compacted force—call it nuclear—of that enigmatic, idealized duality, a democratic culture. Clearly such a culture would be blended, as Williams intuited. Early on, as a young writer tinkering with his name, he signed his first book "William C. Williams." After that, he seriously considered using "W. C. Williams," then finally decided on who he became, defined by the almost comically ordinary and similar first name and last name on either side, escorting between them the central "Carlos." The name is the more American because it is hybrid, implying an immigrant story—the aspiration for a new, mixed, democratic culture.

The history of what I mean is as multiple as the precise yet murky genealogical chains of the Hebrew Bible, that terse geometry of cause and effect, parent and offspring. The minimal, abrupt quality of this one begat that one fascinated me as a child, in Hebrew characters on the right-hand page of the prayer book, with the English on the left.

In Hebrew school, our teacher Mr. Gewirtz divided us eleven- and twelve-year-old students into two teams for the reading-aloud game called Baseball. Saying two lines of Hebrew from the prayer book with no mistakes got you to first base. Mistakes were outs, and stumbles or hesitations were strikes. We knew the meanings of only a few words, so in that competition of phonetic performance, it was all the equivalent of names, Mahalaleel and Methuselah and Japheth. Babbling for perfection was fun. In another way, so was admiring Mr. Gewirtz's mental acrobatics as he defended the idea that in the Torah there were absolutely no contradictions and no mere repetitions.

The begats of weird names living their hundreds of years were scary and funny at once. The stories of all that death and endeavor, coupling and fracture, resemble the jumbled information Williams assembles in his "Dedication for a Plot of Ground." In Genesis, an immense, turbulent flow of lives and deaths has been cooked down to minimal pairs of barely pronounceable names. Sala begat Eber and then he lived four hundred and three years and then he died. The begats mocked and lamented the darkness of actual, real lives, folded away into the shadows of their syllables for centuries.

Those genealogical catalogues gesture at the mostly lethal history behind them—and after them. Some people get killed by Cossacks or Nazis, while their cousins sell eyeglasses or illegal whiskey. The genealogy of causes and effects, along with the curses of recurring genocide, slavery and expropriation, enumerates a history not just of survival (as they taught us in Hebrew school) but of inseparable confusion, beauty and horror.

On Rockwell Avenue, history was a hidden force behind nearly everything—Black and white, Christian and Jew, colors and levels and flavors right in front of me but with unseen causes, authors and consequences. Andy Cullen and Martin Gates lived at the Liberty end of Monmouth Avenue, Dr. McKelvie at the Rockwell end. I had a father and Andy Cullen did not.

Andy's hair was yellow and straight, his cousin Martin's was dark and straight like mine, and Lloyd Weaver's was black, in tight curls. Our Rockwell landlord, Mr. Cutter, slept the night in a toolshed when he came around to collect our rent or putter in the yard. He was someone to be avoided because he was a drunkard and he did not like Jews. Because his nose was red, with hairy yellow pores, I still do not like strawberries.

One day I was sitting on our front steps watching Mr. Cutter digging in the front yard when our elderly neighbor Mrs. Henry walked by. I was about five years old.

"You ought to get him to help you," she said, smiling toward me.

She meant me, the little boy, but Mr. Cutter looked at the house and thought she meant my father.

"No," he said. "You can't get no work out of a Jew."

All of this information had its history, much of it a nightmare and nearly all of it invisible, though I could feel its presence. It was as though Andy and Lloyd and I each knew different secrets, kept in the dark even though we played together most days. Mr. Cutter knew some other secret. Even my parents' arguments about where we lived had their separate histories or secrets: his father's Mob ties, her father's feckless, repeated moves around the country.

A terrifying clot of secrets in the words "Jesus Christ." People said them mostly in anger or shock. Coming from Mr. Cutter they would be pure menace, but in songs called carols and the other songs called spirituals, the words enclosed an elevated sweetness, forbidden to us Jews. Or hidden from us.

Mr. Cutter inherited the Rockwell house from his mother, whose corpse—my mother said—he might have hidden in the immense padlocked travel trunk stored on a ledge above our basement stairway. That seemed unlikely, but possible.

Trying to understand the web of interwoven delusions, stories and realities sometimes led to mistaken ideas. In my family we were Jews and we were all right-handed. The Black kids I knew from Monmouth Avenue also all happened to write and throw as righties. But at school I noticed that a white gentile kid named Jerry Fornin wrote with his left hand. Andy Cullen too was a leftie. So for a little while I thought only certain goyim could be left-handed.

My mother's fantasy about Mr. Cutter's dead mother, like Dr. McKelvie being prevented from swimming at Cramer's Beach, or strawberry-nosed Cutter hating Jews—all of that went deeper than handwriting or swimming, deeper in a way than even hating or dying. Everything came from a nameless, densely crazy power that ruled the world. Even poetry and music, even sex—all were on its dark agenda.

III

Little Egypt

THE TALLY-HO TAVERN once advertised an exotic dancer named Little Egypt. The poster with her picture impressed me. At the age of eleven I understood that the word "Egypt" involved the remote past. I didn't know that for a hundred years dozens of American dancers of different races, mostly strippers or belly dancers, had been billed as "Little Egypt." By the time I was twelve we had moved away from Rockwell and the Tally-Ho Tavern, to Woolley Avenue, near the high school. The two words "Little Egypt" made a thrilling combination of the familiar and the unknown. Sex was only part of it.

Years later, the Coasters had a hit song called "Little Egypt," covered by Elvis Presley. By that time I was at Rutgers, trying to be a poet and to think about an American version of waking up from the nightmare of history. But the nightmare was also alluring. Whoever invented the name "Little Egypt" in the nineteenth century understood its appeal, entangled in the history of girlie shows and the nude, colonialism and exoticism, the male gaze and fetishes. ("She did the hoochie-coochie real slow," sang the Coasters, with the Leiber and Stoller lyrics using another nineteenth century phrase.) As with actual dreams, the horrible and the desired, corruption and culture, were not rationally segregated. Stephen Dedalus's "awakening" might be too simple.

In another way, but also skeptical, I absorbed an idea from a history class: that although we are a great nation, we in the United States had not yet become a great people—still an ongoing effort, with the racial divide only the largest, clearest fracture. Could our public education and our popular culture hold us together in that effort? That would depend upon our works of art, I decided—still that much of a Stephen Dedalus loyalist.

As a college freshman newly converted to Literature with a capital *L*, I became a devotee of Shelley's College Book Store on Somerset Street in New Brunswick. That store advertised "Thousands of books, from 19 cents to $1.98." For a clean used copy of the Laurel paperback edition of Emily Dickinson's poems, introduction by Richard Wilbur, I paid something near the bottom of that price range. Shelley's also sold new books, and I splurged $2.50 on the City Lights edition of *Kaddish and Other Poems* by Allen Ginsberg. Most profound and extravagant of all, I paid Mr. Shelley an almost unthinkable sum (five or six dollars, I think) for a new, hardcover *Collected Poems of William Butler Yeats*, in the Definitive Edition of 1956.

I was ignorant of the actual realities of the book business. I had no idea that books were like movies or music, with the important products being the new releases of each season. That naïveté persisted into my thirties, when I finally learned about the terms "backlist," "remaindered" and "out of print." The presence of a title on Shelley's "used" shelves was evidence, for me, that it might be a significant book—the older and more battered the copy, the more impressive the author might be. Unlike some of my friends, I wasn't mainly interested in what was new. It was freedom of access to the classics that thrilled me.

Orlando Patterson writes about the word "freedom" in relation to the Virginia planters who practiced slavery, and profited from it, and who wrote our founding documents. Did they value the word precisely because "freedom" was a daily, visible denominator for the difference between themselves and the kidnapped African people they had enslaved, and sometimes raped? Patterson has said that in seeking to understand the evil wolf, slavery, he found this unlikely lamb, freedom. The Virginians created, in their own interests and to fill their needs, an intense reimagining that lifted up the very word "freedom." And the enslaved people, trying to awaken from the nightmare, adapted "freedom" and deployed it, as they did Christianity.

Adaptation as distinct from waking up, or as a form of waking up. That idea helps me think about real-life quirks and paradoxes—for instance, Monmouth Avenue, with Little Egypt and Dr. Julius McKelvie at opposite ends of that short street. I can't pretend to analyze its history beyond a misty, almost parodic sense of begats.

The English class system begat dissenting Protestant settlers, who begat profit and enterprise, and profit and enterprise begat settlers and settlers begat colonialism, genocide and slavery. Slavery begat field chants and lynching and field chants begat the blues and the blues begat Duke Ellington and Duke Ellington begat Ella Fitzgerald and John Coltrane and Stan Getz playing Brazilian rhythms with Astrud Gilberto, and the Borscht Belt begat Margaret Cho and Chris Rock. Lynching begat the Southern Strategy of the Republicans. European emigration begat nostalgic yearning and nostalgic yearning begat opera houses and opera houses begat vaudeville and vaudeville begat four-year-old Buster Keaton's father throwing his athletic little child around the stage, and

East Coast entrepreneurs begat Hollywood and Hollywood begat Bollywood long after it begat the grown-up Buster Keaton and the grown-up Buster Keaton begat Jackie Chan years after he begat Sid Caesar and Imogene Coca. Sid Caesar and Imogene Coca begat Carol Burnett and Harvey Korman. In my own microcosm of poetry, T. S. Eliot begat Allen Ginsberg, who wrote imitations of T. S. Eliot and had erotic dreams about him.

When I first discovered Eliot and Ginsberg, in the Beatnik ambience of college, I read their poetry eagerly and thought the two poets were quite similar. Later, in class, I was taught that they were utterly different. A decade or so later, I realized that they were quite similar. Another source of confidence: When I was very young, in our Rockwell Avenue days, my family watched on television Sid Caesar's great parodies of operas and foreign movies, and we laughed at them together. Also, we were not only proud of Count Basie as a native of Monmouth County, we had his records.

That is one piece of evidence for the Pinsky claim that we had good taste. We listened to Basie and Ellington and we watched Sid Caesar. We scorned Lawrence Welk, who triumphed over Caesar broadcasting in the same competitive time slot. I had never seen an opera nor a foreign movie, but I loved the parodies and learned from them something essential about how the world lives in art. From Caesar's doubletalk in Italian, French, Japanese—languages whose melodies he could improvise the more effectively, more purely, because he did not know the languages in the ordinary sense—I learned something essential about language itself.

Who could claim, when Ellington and Keaton were new, to know that their art was great?

Who could predict that *Sherlock Jr.*, and "Black and Tan Fantasy" would come to be curated by American universities? Also, Bert Williams and Groucho Marx, along with William Carlos Williams. Who knows nowadays which hip-hop performers or which contemporary writers for television, or which contemporary poets, will be so honored by the generation currently about to enter kindergarten? Who cares? In fact, I do—I care, even though I can't pretend to know. And there are experts who do know, or will.

Or is it too sunny, too optimistic on my part to concentrate on the historic work of Ellington and Keaton and the scholarly caretakers of their art? Is it a sad, terrible doom that their work now rests—as in mausoleums—in universities? Or, after all, a hopeful indication that American culture is democratic and scholarly, both: that it embraces Ellington's music and Keaton's films, available to the generations, as Joyce and Dickinson were available to me when I was seventeen?

Or is it more important to realize how much bad has always come along with the good? The culture, along with producing Emily Dickinson and Sid Caesar and T. S. Eliot and Allen Ginsberg and George Gershwin and Willa Cather and Preston Sturges and Elizabeth Bishop and John Coltrane and Nina Simone and Richard Pryor and Gwendolyn Brooks and Mel Brooks and Robert Hayden and Stanley Kubrick also produced a stupendous, toxic flood of vulgarity. Is it more to the point that the Great Depression begat radio quiz shows like *Queen for a Day*, and *Queen for a Day* on radio begat *This Is Your Life* on television, and *This Is Your Life* begat a family named Loud that begat "reality" television that begat big-time professional wrestling and big-time professional wrestling begat *The Apprentice* that begat President Donald J. Trump?

Or not? Don't ask me, I am tempted to say, I just write poems. I am an expert at nothing except the sounds of sentences in the English language. My translation *The Inferno of Dante* is not an accomplishment of scholarship. It tries to be a feat of metrical engineering. Composed with the instrument of my voice, intended for any reader's voice. Poetry. That peculiar form of musical composition in speakable words, an ancient bodily and imaginative art, doesn't confer the power to know which American creations are great and which are just plausible, or worse. If the Dante translation works as art, then like my poems and all of my writing it is part of an American process of adaptation and adoption. (Some might call it "appropriation.")

For me, that uncertain sense of still making up the culture as we go along adds to the thrill of poetry as an American art. I used to hear people talk enviously about poetry in the Soviet Union. They marveled at those soccer stadiums where poets declaimed their poems in the flamboyant Russian style to audiences of tens of thousands. I never was impressed. In a culture where poetry had long-established snob value and "you have no culture" is an insult, promotion by the Soviet Ministry of Culture was the equivalent of support from Coca-Cola or 20th Century Fox. As to those tens of thousands of Soviet citizens in soccer stadiums, buying established, state-supported baloney—who cares? I prefer our tentative, impro-vised, still-to-be-created, self-critical scene, even with its idiotic fads and gaffes.

I'd rather compose my work in a culture where poetry is still being defined—even where (I've heard) some academ-ics try to make students choose between Walt Whitman and Emily Dickinson.

IV

Change Trains at Summit

USED TO follow the self-imposed rule that you should not presume to call yourself a poet. "It's for the world to say," said Robert Frost. So for years, even after I began publishing my work, I would avoid "I am a poet" and say instead, "I write poems."

But in the meantime the exalted word "poet" went its own way, becoming more and more a term for all kinds of things, including an academic job category. ("We need to hire a poet.")

Following Frost's principle started to feel like an affectation. His cunning declaration that "poet" is something for other people to say was like him: the modest surface and the covert, underlying superiority. There's also a bit of superstition involved—bad luck to claim the word for yourself. That backspin has its appeal. But a couple of books into my career I let myself say out loud, at times, that I was a poet.

It wasn't modesty that drove me to shy away from using the word about myself. Deep down, it wasn't just Robert Frost either, but a matter of where I came from—a quiet, stubborn and provincial pride in what you are and shame at the very idea of pretending to be anything you might not be. Where I grew up, it might be fine to be a poet, though possibly less valuable than to be an optometrist. In certain limited ways, it might even be acceptable to be a criminal. What was not acceptable was vaunting bullshit about yourself. "Poet" was a great thing to me—none greater, really, so not to be desecrated.

Even saying "I write poems" is inaccurate. "Write" is not precise. What I work to produce is not marks on paper, but something more like a song or a monologue, or both. I was never that precocious child or teenager who, to a family's pride and admiration, would sit down to produce work on a page with pen or a typewriter.

All respect to that precociously literary, seated child whose story I have often read or heard. The image has been genuine many times, I know, and not always like the bad-faith scene Jean-Paul Sartre describes from his early childhood: little Jean-Paul bent over a big, difficult book in his grandfather's study, intensely aware of the admiration he was courting from his onlookers, the awed servants and his mother.

I know that there are people who think by writing. None of us is purely one thing, but I tend to think by speaking, often to myself. Even now, as all my life, my poems don't usually begin on paper, or on a screen. It's a matter of humming and muttering, grunts and echoes in the vowels and consonants of speech, the melody of every sentence. I get a tune in my head. Toying with bits of remembered conversation, maybe half-remembered lines by Keats or Dickinson mixed with a joke or a bit of gossip, is like noodling at the piano. Sometimes you discover something new.

Early on, it seemed like a bad habit, a nervous tic. I remember gently rapping the sounds of sentences on my headboard, in the dark, with drumming fingers. Possibly I did that in my crib. I thought about how pitch affected rhythm, and about the harmonies or discords of consonants. At night, before I fell asleep I listened to the voices in my head, not for their meaning but for their shapes. It was a compulsion, like chewing your fingernails. At its most useful, a way of memorizing phone numbers, each with its unique tune.

I thought about things like how saying the first *s* in "sounds" didn't vibrate in my throat, but the second *s* did, and how in the same way mouthing the *th* in "think" didn't vibrate there but the *th* in "the" did. Noticing such things felt like a minor but distinct mental disorder I would have to live with. Many years later I learned the terminology for what I heard: voiced and unvoiced consonants. Voiced and unvoiced. I had thought the difference was my own invention or delusion, but people had studied it. There were words for it, which made it real.

I thought about "scarf" and "carve" and how those words were fun to say for the contrast between the *k* sound happening way in the back of my mouth and the *v* or *f* sound in the extreme front, teeth on lower lip. In the words of the song "Open the Door, Richard" I liked how the *r* sound at the end of a slow word became the *r* sound at the beginning of a fast word.

"Passengers going to Hoboken, change trains at Summit" is an example of sentence melody: those three triplets at the beginning, each slower than the one before, the name of the New Jersey city so much slower than the same rhythm in "passengers." Then the long pair of "change trains" followed by the quick little Dizzy Gillespie fillip with a second place-name "at Summit." Chanting it over to myself, playing its rhythm in my mind against a 4/4 time signature, listening for the relation of pitch and length to cadence, immersed in all that, I might get so distracted that I forgot to change trains.

So as a kid I didn't exactly write poems, but in my mind's ear I did compose them. As models I had the folklore of alternative lyrics. To the tune of a commercial jingle, "Pepsi-Cola is the drink / To pour down the kitchen sink. / Tastes like vinegar, looks like ink— / Pepsi-Cola is sure to stink." To the tune of "Jealousy," "Leprosy." ("There goes my eyeball / Into your highball.") Anonymous parodies and pastiches like that were easy to pick up at school, and I became an expert.

When the excellent Mill Valley Public Library in California asked me to suggest a short poem to be projected onto their footpath, I proposed a great folk poem I learned and admired when I was ten years old. It was composed by some soldier or series of soldiers in World War II, building on the information that Adolf Hitler suffered from an undescended testicle. It can be sung to the tune of the "Colonel Bogey March":

> Hitler
> Has only got one ball.
>
> Goering
> Has two, but very small.
>
> Himmler
> Has something similar,
>
> And Goebbels
> Has no balls
> At all.

This brilliant bit of rudeness is a marvel of economy. The rhyming of "Himmler" and "similar" encourages playing with an accent. The imperfect rhyming of "Goebbels" and "no balls" adds to the insolence, with the triumphant final rhyme. I can't hear the "Colonel Bogey" tune without thinking of those lyrics. (The soldiers in *The Bridge on the River*

Kwai must be thinking them while they whistle them for their captors, Hitler's allies in the Pacific.)

An anonymous, funny, anti-Fascist poem seemed to me a patriotic selection. But possibly offensive to some. Wisely, the Mill Valley librarian asked me for a safer choice, and we settled on Emily Dickinson's "Fame Is a Fickle Food."

I am not talking about dramatic vocal performances of poetry, still less about academic notions of poems as graphic presences on a page. A few years ago there was an interesting New York poetry series called "Page and Stage," bringing together two poets, one in each category. They invited me to appear in either category I chose. My honest answer was that my gifts and interests were neither Stage nor Page. If I give a poetry reading I hope not to bore the audience, and when I publish a book I hope the poems will look inviting in print. But the medium I write for is not performance and not paper, but any reader's actual or imagined voice.

For me, poetry is a vocal art but not necessarily a performer's art. I compose poems with my voice, for your voice. It's all in the sounds written into the words—free verse or in meter, rhymed or not. The great demonstration of what I mean is in the online videos made for the Favorite Poem Project.

In those videos, the voices of readers fulfill the art of consonant and vowel, sentence and cadence, created by poets. As Sylvia Plath is to the Jamaican immigrant who reads Plath's poem "Nick and the Candlestick," or as Langston Hughes is to the Cambodian American high school student who reads his "Minstrel Man" or as Walt Whitman is to the construction worker who reads from "Leaves of Grass"—that, to me, is the highest and most essential ambition in poetry. That another person wants to give voice to your exact words.

I was invited to a forum called "On the Humanities." Our moderator, a decent man who had been a college president, commented on the small vocabulary of a proto-fascist American politician. The politician's speeches, said our moderator, used a remarkably limited vocabulary. His electoral success was, therefore, a mystery.

That good, well-intentioned man, the head of a major foundation, knows a lot more than I do about politics, money, governance. How could he be so naïve about odious but successful rhetoric? Had his ear been deadened by the prose of scholars and officials? As an American humanist he needed to hear, in his generation and mine, the comic George Carlin commenting on the jargon of Washington politicians who never *say* but "indicate," never *decide* but "determine," never *do* but "proceed" and so forth—a language the demagogue knew how to avoid, undermine and mock with one-syllable words. The limited vocabulary helped energize what a writer I know has called "charismatic indecency."

My college president friend needed to appreciate the profound understanding of sentence sounds in the work of Richard Pryor or Elmore Leonard. In the conversation at that forum on the humanities, the nominal subject was a disaster in American politics. The underlying issue was a failure to comprehend American culture—as an unfinished, defective and sometimes glorious project, with its erratic orbit between the cross-fertilized poles of democratic genius and populist vulgarity.

I was blessed by growing up within a certain version of what can be called an "oral tradition." A network of personal, offhanded wisecracks and casual performances inspired me with those rhymed compositions at the expense of the drink Pepsi-Cola or the Nazi propaganda master Dr. Goebbels. "Tastes like ink" and "no balls at all" have their musical meanings.

Maybe I should be grateful I was born to parents who were not college-trained in the spirit of that humanities forum, but verbally gifted, and that we lived in a community of various immigrants on the border of a Black neighborhood. There was a tradition behind Muhammad Ali's saying he could murder a brick and "I'm so mean, I make medicine sick." I had the good luck to be raised among expert joke-tellers, complainers, arguers, schmoozers, boasters and liars.

As I make that list with "liars" at the end, I realize that I am echoing a comic style, the inverted swagger of my parents and their friends. I was born into a little-known social class, a provincial, small-town, or neighborhood American gentility who have been in one place for a generation or two. We come from various religions and skin tones, we may have grandparents who are migrants or dirt farmers, but we are confident frogs in the little ponds we inherit or devise. We know who we are, and we recognize one another at a glance, or inside a few seconds of conversation, even across different regional accents or other divides.

Or am I talking about a period of time, not just of geography and social setting? Am I talking about, or speaking for, a twentieth century kind of American, deceased FDR voters and their surviving children and grandchildren? Whoever we are, we tell jokes we call dirty and we also share a complicated pleasure in measuring when it is more effective to say "baloney" than "bullshit." We have our artistry, manners, obligations, defects and customs, at least as distinct a group as the people likely to display what they consider a high-class college name on the rear windows of their minivans.

From that kind of academic or social pretension, and (let's hope) from literary pretension as well, I have been protected by what you might call advantages of birth, in my family's segment of what the ignorant might call the lower middle class.

I will try to be specific.

V

The Aristocratic Principle

MILFORD SIMON PINSKY, my father, went to college for a couple of weeks. Some people might say it wasn't a real college, only what was called "night school." Monmouth Junior College didn't have a campus or a building of its own. Classes took place after working hours, in the familiar rooms and hallways of Long Branch High School, where my father and I both graduated, as did my mother, my brother and sister and our many cousins. So too did my aunts and uncles.

I don't know how Monmouth managed to change in my lifetime from that night-school community junior college to Monmouth University, with its national opinion polls and its elegant, ever-expanding campus. I remember the old days of Shadow Lawn, the Guggenheim estate that became the central heart of Monmouth University. The building housed Highland Manor, a private school for girls. When I was at Long Branch High, I was recruited—how, maybe through a music teacher?—to put on a necktie and attend dances there a few times. The experience of dancing with rich girls was enhanced by the surroundings, which seemed like something from the movies, by far the grandest rooms I had ever been in.

Ivy-covered swags of steel chain used to loop gracefully between stone columns in a long wall separating Highland Manor, in the old Guggenheim estate, from the traffic on Westwood Avenue. It looked eternal, but the wall and chains came down and the property was inherited by Monmouth Junior College. The nickname for Monmouth University teams is the Hawks—which harks back to the Night Hawks of the old days when the college classes met after dark, in Long Branch High School.

My father and I had the same homeroom teacher, Miss Scott. Milford Pinsky played baseball, football and basketball. In the senior poll for the class of 1934, he was voted Best-Looking Boy, a bit of recognition he enjoyed and did not forget. (Twenty-four years later my classmates elected me Most Musical Boy, a title less deserved than his.)

My mother enjoyed her husband's Best-Looking title too, in her own ironic, teasing way. For Sylvia Pinsky, as for the most ambitious poets and stand-up comedians, no subject was forbidden. For a few years after the Nazis lost the war, mystery surrounded the fate of Adolf Hitler. His suicide in an underground bunker was for a long time just one rumor among rumors, not yet documented. Was Hitler hiding in Paraguay or South Africa? Or maybe he had plastic surgery, then got himself smuggled into the United States? He could be anywhere, even on the New Jersey Shore, dropped off by a U-boat in the middle of the night onto some secluded landing in Sea Bright or Port-au-Peck.

The fantastic possibilities were a rich mine for speculation, and also for comedy. I remember my mother more than once pinching a little of her long dark hair and holding it under her husband's handsome nose. It was a routine. Cuddling with her legs on his lap, with her free hand she brushed his hair flat onto his forehead above one eye.

"Everybody's looking for Hitler," she said, making the

mustache with the bit of her hair, "and all the time, here he is in Long Branch."

I was five or six years old, but I sort of understood that outrageous, weirdly flirtatious joke. His nervous, protesting laughter voiced a bewildering element that I can identify now as sexual. But in some sense I got the idea even back then. My mother was making my father laugh in a nervous, uncomfortable way: a teasing, I partly understood, that he also enjoyed. Her confident, ruthless defiance of good taste excited him and impressed me. I was proud of their games, and a little scared by them. As an only child until I was six, I got to witness this kind of emotional dance—their laughing tango—at a peak of its intensity.

With the same kind of half understanding, I got the point when Sylvia said that in her husband's family he and the other kids most of the time couldn't use their bathtub, because their father was using it for making gin. Like her saucy appropriation of Adolf Hitler, this taunt about Prohibition brought the lore of history into her marriage's boomerangs of anger and attraction, ridicule and arousal—also, our family's social failings and aspirations. Dave Pinsky, Milford's father, had worked as a driver and soldier for the famous crime kingpin of Newark, Longie Zwillman. ("Longie" from the Yiddish word for "tall.") Dave was a criminal, but the father of a respectable optician.

I'll repeat the important distinction: Opticians make and sell eyeglasses. Optometrists study for an OD degree, qualifying them to project the eye chart and ask you if the letters become more clear or less as they flip lenses. An ophthalmologist, considered the highest category of the three, is a medical doctor who specializes in care of the eyes. Optometrists write prescriptions for corrective lenses: a profession. Opticians like Milford Pinsky practice a trade, grinding lenses and dispensing eyeglasses.

Like many others in that generation of the Great Depression, my father got into his life's work by chance. He was in high school. The teacher in a twelfth-grade study hall read a notice: Anyone interested in becoming an apprentice optician could be interviewed after school by the optometrist Dr. Alexander Vineberg. My father thought the job had to do with teeth, not eyes, he told me.

He and his friend Herbie Grossman decided to go for it. As they left the school for the walk downtown to Dr. Vineberg's office, Milford asked Herbie if he would mind stopping at Milford's house on the way, so Milford could put on a clean shirt. So Herbie waited while Milford changed to a nice shirt, washed his face, and combed his hair. For the rest of their lives, the two men joked that their careers were set that day by Milford's shirt. Herbie remained in town, with his hardware store on Broadway a few doors away from the office of Alexander Vineberg, OD.

Besides making and selling eyeglasses, an optician also adjusts metal or plastic eyeglass frames. You grip the sidepieces at the hinge with needle-nose pliers, to bend them gently toward a place behind the ear. The front should be slightly bowed inward, and the frame should stay level, not rocking, when you place it, with both sidepieces extended, onto a flat surface. Plastic frames were gently heated for a few seconds in a hot plate full of warm salt. My father would lift a frame from the salt, tweak the softened plastic expertly, then dip it into a tray of cool, soapy water. Polishing the lenses with a lintless towel draped over his shoulder, he settled the frame with professional assurance onto the customer's head.

As he gently eased the eyeglass frames into position, my mother said, if the patient was a woman he might brush her earlobes with his fingertips for a moment as he asked solicitously, looking into her eyes: "How does that feel?"

Not true, of course. Like her Hitler joke, this was a characteristic tease, with Sylvia Pinsky proud of her husband's charm while subverting him. Her love banter brought him to a state wavering, for him, between embarrassment and laughter, and for her, between cruelty and tribute. She repeated her material like the stand-up comics of those days, with variations for different settings. For example, she told the same "how does it feel" story about their friend Walter Holtz, with the woman as a customer in Walter's shoe store, and ankles rather than earlobes.

Another way to look at her teasing, I think, is that it vented her frustrations as a woman of her time and place. She told me that when she was a kid growing up in Little Rock, Arkansas, she was a "tomboy." Here in the twenty-first century, that old-fashioned word might suggest she was gay, but I don't think so. It meant something more complicated than that, a many-sided resistance to social patterns, not only sexual ones. She was athletic, smart, outspoken, with repeated stories of her role as the physically aggressive protector of her younger brother Julian, known as Julie.

In one story, shortly after they had moved from Little Rock to Kansas City, some local boys in the street were tormenting a cat. When Julie asked the boys to stop hurting the animal, they started to shove him around and threaten him. As she tells the story, Sylvia ran downstairs from their apartment and chased those boys away, literally kicking an ass or two. She was specific with details and place names like Kansas City. Unlike us, her husband and children, she was not a small-town provincial. She landed in Long Branch High School at the end of an American wander-tale. Sylvia Eisenberg was born in Little Rock, Arkansas.

As she tells it, her father, Morris Eisenberg, came into Little Rock on his motorcycle and took her mother Becky away from a much older first husband. Becky had a daughter from that first marriage. Sylvia could remember learning how to brush her teeth from her older sister Pearl. Then one day she said goodbye to her sister forever, when the family went to see Pearl off at the station in Little Rock, where the older sister got on a train by herself.

The first marriage, the abandoned child, the motorcycle, Arkansas—these stories let me know that the past is disorderly, exotic, brutal and fascinating. Like the assassination of President Garfield, and the special train that brought him to Long Branch after he was shot, the lost Pearl had her place in a crazy, ongoing story. My grandmother Becky, who often took care of me, amplified my sense of the world as ghost-ridden. She was kind. She spoke English with a Southern accent and Yiddish with a Romanian accent. In both languages her speech sometimes reflected the prejudices of her time. She referred to Italian people as "lokshens" (noodles), and she addressed her beloved, good-looking son-in-law Milford Pinsky, affectionately, as "poylishe chazer" (Polish pig, but with the sweetening irony of Yiddish).

With their mother Becky and their motorcycle-riding father Morris, Sylvia and Julie grew up moving from city to city, with one idyllic year at their maternal grandfather's place in Portland, Oregon. Mostly, the family moved around the country, in the period phrase my mother liked to use, "one jump ahead of the sheriff," until they landed in Long Branch.

I knew my grandfather, Morris Eisenberg, as a part-time junk man and ragpicker and venetian blind installer. For a time he had a window-washing business, taking his bucket and long-handled squeegee to the display windows of stores on Broadway. He was also a part-time tailor, and would occasionally trim hair in his backyard, using his clippers and scissors on men from our shul, the Congregation Brothers of Israel. Given the unsettled variety of his trades, if Morris Eisenberg were a poet, he might be called "experimental."

The motorcycle was long gone, but Morris remained a lover of machines and gadgets. I called him Zaydee, Yiddish for "Grandpa." And since my father called his father "Pop," I called Dave, the much more secular of my two grandfathers—possibly at my mother's suggestion, with her intention to annoy him—"Zaydee Pop."

After being one jump ahead of the sheriff in Morris's unsettled household, it's easy to imagine that for my mother life with a handsome, earnest small-town boy would feel, at least at first, like an escape from instability. But as the traditional roles of wife and mother closed around the former tomboy, it might have felt like a cage. Her charged, sexualized teasing may have included a thwarted hunger for escape.

Joking and sexy teasing, feigned and actual love-anger, are deeply related to the sources of poetry. When I began reading the exaggerated, often hostile courtship display of sixteenth century sonnets, I recognized something fundamental. "Three sorts of serpent do resemble thee," begins a sonnet by Michael Drayton, catching his beloved's attention with a showy attack. "O cunning love," says Shakespeare, "with tears thou keep'st me blind, / Lest eyes, well seeing, thy foul faults should find." Drayton in his poem is not simply angry or insulting any more than Shakespeare simply finds "foul faults" in his lover. They are showing off their eloquence in a poetic peacock-display, with insult as a traditional come-on. An ancient game of erotic flattery-by-insult is at work in the smirking, male aggression of "serpent" and "foul faults." Sylvia's derisive flirting with Milford reversed those traditional gender roles. In the sonneteer flashes and swerves of her wit, he was like the fair yet unfair maiden.

It's possible that Milford's good looks also had something to do with how his night school career at Monmouth Junior College ended so soon after it began. The course was English Composition. The first assignment was to write a paragraph defining some important word or idea. My father chose to write a definition of the word "gentleman."

At the next meeting of Composition after he submitted his paper "What Is a Gentleman?" the professor asked for Milford Pinsky to please stay on after class for a conference—a kind of attention far from routine at the homeless, more or less free, community-college Monmouth of those days.

When the two of them were alone in that familiar, repurposed high school classroom, my father's first college professor accused him of plagiarism. Where, in what book, the professor seated at the teacher's desk wanted to know, did Milford find these sentences to copy? My father's answer was:

"I didn't copy it, I wrote it."

The teacher did not believe him, which may mean that the essay was well written.

Maybe my father's reputation as an athlete, along with his physical appearance and something in his manner, also made that night school English teacher skeptical. The poet Mark Strand once confided to me, with a chuckle, that he thought his reputation as a male beauty, so often written about or gossiped about, had been more of a disadvantage than an asset in his literary career. Mark found this perception funny, one more example of the literary world's dopiness.

Another quality Mark Strand shared with my father is that they knew how to laugh at themselves. That kind of humor is the opposite, in my experience, of egotistical. But the trouble with self-deprecating comedy is that many dull people understand it merely as deprecation. Humorless people take the self-mockery of others literally. I think both men, in their quite different ways, suffered from that.

What my father wrote in that first English Composition assignment, he told me, was that a gentleman can be defined as someone more concerned about the well-being of other people than about his own. I hear an accidental literary echo in that definition. Quite possibly my father never heard of Henry James. I am certain he never read James's novel *Por-*

trait of a Lady, where James writes about his heroine Isabel Archer that she "solemnly pondered" to herself:

> " . . . that's the supreme good fortune: to be in a better position for appreciating people than they are for appreciating you." And she added that such, when one considered it, was simply the essence of the aristocratic situation. In this light, if none other, one should aim at the aristocratic situation.

Could it be that the night school professor was thinking about this passage, and concluded that young Milford Pinsky had stolen from it? Associating generous character with gentility, the idea that classiness is the best meaning of class: That notion, pondered solemnly by James's fictional young heroine in her innocence, was part of my father's upbringing, or anyway of his social world. Possibly buried in their bad encounter and that definition of "gentleman" there is a compliment to the teacher, the student, and their times. Nowadays, it's likely that neither student nor teacher would have read *Portrait of a Lady*. In a way, the accusation of plagiarism was flattering.

As my father told the story, he never returned to that classroom, or to Monmouth or any other college. As an explanation for dropping out of school forever, this account is true as far as it goes, but maybe too neat. In the middle of the Great Depression, there were plenty of other reasons, beyond offended innocence, to drop out of English Composition in particular and higher education in general. A steady, paying job mattered more.

And he did have a steady job for ten years, beginning in high school, from the day he raised his hand in study hall. In the rear workroom of Dr. Vineberg's office, my father made and repaired eyeglasses as an apprentice optician. He passed the state exam and progressed to helping customers choose frames while he sat across a table from them, wearing what was then the customary white lab coat, collarless and buttoned high at the neck. I can remember being glad to have a task in that workroom when I was five or six years old. They gave me a box of snap-open eyeglass cases, and I fitted inside the upper lid of each one a business card: "Alexander Vineberg, O.D."

Vineberg in my memory would suit the old-fashioned word "portly." The optometrist wore not a lab coat like my optician father but a suit and tie. My impression of him as genial but a bit scary may come not from experience, but from the fact that he fired my father—"let him go" was the expression. His boss wished Milford well, he explained, but Dr. Vineberg was planning to run for mayor of Long Branch, and it would be wise, in 1947, for a Jewish candidate to hire a war veteran from an Italian family. There may be more to the story, but that outline as it came down to me still seems plausible.

At seven years old, I was just barely able to get the idea of losing a job. All the adults involved seemed to know and accept a lot of mysterious forces: the mayoral election, the Italian veteran, the Jewish optometrist, the "letting go." Dr. Vineberg's plan succeeded. He was elected mayor. Junior Schiavone, the veteran he hired, learned the trade and worked at Dr. Vineberg's as an optician for years. My father and Junior both showed some class, my father in helping Junior learn the job, and Junior reciprocating in various little ways over the years. They were on the same bowling team.

Showing some class was an idea shared by Italian, Irish, Jewish, Black and white Protestant families in our town. But those useful labels are clumsy. Some of them include too much or too little, and some of them in particular are not right for that time and place, where the respectful word for Black people was "colored"; Protestants would likely be referred to as "American" or maybe "just American." "WASP" was a term I heard for the first time in college.

And of course there was the large vocabulary of slurs and insults. Some of those bad words, like "queer" in the twenty-first century, might be defiantly taken over by the target group. "Micks don't eat that stuff," I can remember Jimmy Clancy saying about Chinese food.

In that same local vocabulary, the language of my childhood, the phrases "high class," "no class," "low class," "showing a little class" and "classy" had distinct shades of meaning and sub-tones, contradictory but powerful. To be both noble and egalitarian was not just possible but desirable, fitting into an outlook that was both aristocratic and egalitarian. Junior Schiavone and my father, showing some class, behaved like gentlemen.

I don't exactly remember my father coming home to 36 Rockwell Avenue and breaking the news that he had been "let go" by Vineberg. But I do have some vivid memories from the time, of my parents' shouting arguments about money or about our living in that "slum." At one especially loud, angry moment my father took out his wallet—maybe he knew he had a lot of singles—and threw what I remember as a cascade or blizzard of paper money, which drifted down all over the kitchen.

"Is this what you want?" he yelled. "You want money? Here, help yourself!"

As a seven-year-old I was used to their lurches between rage and laughter. I remember dashing around and grabbing some of the bills while the two of them laughed, the three of us dissolving maniacally into the moment.

After an anxious month or two, my father opened his own business, of a kind Long Branch had not seen before. An optician's office. Since he could not examine eyes, the enterprise would not work unless people who had seen medical doctors brought him eyeglass prescriptions to fill. The names of local ophthalmologists—Dr. Strauss, Dr. Ciampa, Dr. London,

Dr. Niederhoffer—had the mystical weight of ancient capricious gods. Some of them asked for kickbacks, money paid for every patient they sent to the optician. Shrewd and moralistic, the gentle former Boy Scout Milford Pinsky politely declined to make those payments—and, in one of his favored expressions, it all worked out okay.

For my eighth birthday my parents gave me a pair of Bushnell binoculars my father got from a lens wholesaler he did business with—bottom of the manufacturer's line, as I realized much later, but I loved them. I liked using them both ways, to make whatever I looked at appear large and close, or small and remote.

VI

Partnership

SOON AFTER he opened his own business, my father took a partner, a tall, meticulous, baldheaded optometrist named P. Kirk Pettiford. The two of them pooled a little start-up money—it might have been as small as a thousand dollars each, my father's share borrowed. He had no collateral, but the officer at the bank, John Smock, was a former basketball teammate who okayed Milford Pinsky as "a Long Branch boy." In a phrase of that time, John Smock gave Milford a break. It was a New Jersey break, in the sense not necessarily of a this-for-that, but recognizing possible favors, past or future, in a communal network.

Kirk Pettiford was from another state. He was a craftsman of a limited but elegant kind. He had a lovely handwriting and he created a handsome, professional-looking sign for their business, a horizontal plywood panel with a dark green background and gold letters: "Milford S. Pinsky, Optician" and "P. Kirk Pettiford, Optometrist," with a vertical gold line precisely in the center, separating the two names. Possibly "Pinsky" came first as a courtesy on Kirk's part, or as a recognition of the "Long Branch boy" factor. His competence using tools interested me, as so different from the Pinsky talents of a more theatrical kind. His name, neither Jewish nor Italian, also had a rare, almost exotic distinction.

The partnership was a new battlefield. My mother suspected that Kirk Pettiford was taking advantage of her gullible husband, who at some point said to her—or anyway she quoted him repeatedly as saying—"Right now, Kirk needs more cash than I do." How he must have regretted saying anything like that!

At some point Kirk tried to defend himself to Sylvia directly, explaining to her that he was a Methodist, which required that he always be fair and honest in everything he did. She was outraged by that religious argument, and often quoted it scornfully. "The Methodical Methodist" was one of her more polite nicknames for Kirk.

But the partnership prospered. The systematic, reticent optometrist performed vision exams in the dark side-room with the projected eye charts. He impressed and amused his optician partner by taking far longer than Dr. Vineberg ever did to complete each examination. In keeping with my mother's nickname for him, the Methodical Optometrist wrote extremely legible, double-checked prescriptions to be filled by the personable optician, who helped their customers choose eyeglass frames from display cases in the front room. During those partnership years, I helped out in the backroom workshop, tidying up and emptying into the toilet the milky-looking waste water from buckets kept under the lens-grinding machines. I even learned to do minor repairs on eyeglass frames.

It was also my assignment to organize the waiting room magazines. Pinsky and Pettiford subscribed to *Life*, *Look*, *McCall's*, *Time*, and the *Saturday Evening Post*. The different styles of graphic authority, fresh every week, fascinated me. The word "art" still meant things like the leafy and floral borders someone had painted on the mirrors in Sam Serge's Sanitary Barber Shop, across Broadway from the Pinsky/Pettiford office. But in that bygone age of paper, the slick magazines—that was the adjective used in the trade, based on the glossy paper—were a doorway to the world. Magazines brought works of art into millions of lives, including mine.

I admired the *Saturday Evening Post* covers by Norman Rockwell and the *Life* photographs by (though I didn't know their names) Margaret Bourke-White, Robert Capa, Gordon Parks and others. The waiting room magazines also contained writing, including fiction and light verse. I read sea adventure stories by C. S. Forester and cowboy stories by Zane Grey and poems by Ogden Nash. Possibly I also read fiction by Ray Bradbury, William Faulkner, Ernest Gaines and Ernest Hemingway in the *Post*, a magazine allegedly "founded by Benjamin Franklin," as a subhead boasted above those Norman Rockwell cover images. I appreciated the comic poetry by Nash and his competitors in that obsolete category.

Possibly I read poetry or prose written by Dorothy Parker, who, as it happens—yet another thing I did not know at the time—was born in Long Branch, in 1893, when her name was Dorothy Rothschild. In that field of mostly white, Christian, male authors she would fit into only one of those three categories.

Rockwell's cover paintings, brilliant fantasies of everyday American life, commanded attention. Even kids knew that "Norman Rockwell," pronounced with varying tones of mockery and admiration, was shorthand for something—something that made nearly all of us Americans wonder, were we American enough? The paintings intimidated and beckoned us with hyper-reality and hyper-normality, in an unnatural, perfected clarity of detail and behavior. They were as clear and emphatic as the adventure hero comic books forbidden in Sylvia Pinsky's household. Like the comic-book images available in other kids' houses, Rockwell's covers generated the thrills of anxiety and exaggeration.

Could children feel the social anxiety implicit in Rockwell's appealing images? Of course we did, like everybody else. The coincidence that we lived on Rockwell Avenue didn't seem odd. The street's name, in contrast with our neighborhood of boardinghouses and multi-family conversions, Black people and white, suggested a past when the name "Rockwell" was part of a bygone purity, when the town was less mixed. The same name for our mixed, declining street as for the painter of a pure, idealized elsewhere, familiar yet unattained, would have made sense if I had thought about it. (In fact, Colonel A. F. Rockwell was at Lincoln's deathbed. A close friend of President Garfield, the Rockwell our street was named for fought in the Civil War under Grant.)

Growing up in a historic, perpetually declining American resort town, with families of year-round Hispanic and South Asian newcomers beginning to arrive, I could see that nearly everybody feels like an outsider, one way or another. In school we learned about the Lenni Lenape who bargained with the first European settlers for as much land as one of them walked off in a day, creating the shape of Long Branch. Maybe I would have understood the words on a twenty-first century T-shirt: "This Is America—Speak Navajo."

Summer people as outsiders were different from us year-round people. In another kind of difference, people with names that sounded Italian or Jewish or Irish or Puerto Rican were outsiders, distinct from people with names that sounded (like Rockwell) "American." From their own viewpoint—a child could understand this—in our immigrant-filled land they might feel more like outsiders than anyone else, as the roots of xenophobia and nativism keep refreshing their toxic blossoms.

The earnest, innocent Methodist Kirk Pettiford may have

felt like an outsider in our town. A shy, nervous man might notice his difference from the sociable Long Branch boy Milford Pinsky. He knew that the name "Pettiford" on the elegant sign he had crafted would not be familiar to people who drank at Dave Pinsky's bar or had gone to high school with Milford. Milford, on the other hand, had to be aware that the name "Pinsky" on that handcrafted sign meant that he was a Jew—that is, not a member of the majority religion with its Christian music and architecture, its all but universal images and its dictionary.

I didn't know that Robert Capa was a Hungarian immigrant who had fled the rise of Fascism in Europe. I didn't know that Gordon Parks was a Black man. But if I did have the information, by the age of ten or eleven I would already have gotten the general idea that immigrants and the descendants of enslaved Africans occupied distinct, risky social places. There were concentration camp survivors in town, and living on Rockwell Avenue gave me daily, immediate evidence of the vicious American racial setup.

It was clear and a little bewildering that skin color dictated a different life from mine, present and future, for the Rockwell-Monmouth neighborhood kids I played with—Billy Hanford, Lloyd Weaver, Ronnie and Juanita Dupuis, Clifford Little, Grady Best. Every year as we got older the difference between white and Black, sometimes nearly invisible (but not on the segregated beaches) when we were small, got bigger and more severe. When we were all in kindergarten, not much apparent difference. By the fifth grade, a lot of difference, and a few years later puberty made the gulf immense.

Our segregated beaches, representing so much, add a different overtone to a sentence I heard thousands of times growing up: "The town isn't what it used to be." As with the old joke about "They don't make movies like they used to anymore," one might add, "Thank God!" Or, "I hope not."

"The town isn't what it used to be." The statement might mean little to a newcomer like Kirk Pettiford, but the words were so familiar it was as if they appeared on the Long Branch city flag. Hearing the saying repeatedly as a child led to a romantic and misinformed blur—was it a lament for the recent beach erosion and this year's slow summer for the tourist hotels? Or was "not what it used to be" about the century before, when presidents and celebrities came to the town?

"America's First Seashore Resort" said the billboard-sized sign on Broadway, just above a creek next to the bar owned by Dave Pinsky's onetime partner in crime, Izzy Schneider. "First" might aspire to meaning "in the lead" but clearly it meant "a long time ago." The general, civic mourning—for a past tourist season or for a past century—fostered a rich confusion about degrees of remoteness in time, overlapping epochs of nostalgic losses and diminishing glory. Nothing is more elegiac than a seashore boardwalk in winter.

Winslow Homer's painting *Long Branch, New Jersey*, with the two women in gowns and bustles, with their little dog, on the high bluff above the beach below, hangs in Boston's Museum of Fine Arts. Homer made many engravings of the town's summer crowds for *Harper's* magazine.

The old, fading American upper class summered in Saratoga Springs, New York, for the racetrack and the medicinal springs, or they went to Newport, Rhode Island, for the boating and the ocean breezes. That elite social world of debutantes and exclusive clubs was being overwhelmed by the show business luminaries and patent-medicine millionaires who came to Long Branch, where the new, all-conquering idea of celebrity was invented.

I talk about the town too much, I have heard, and I know too much about it. There's an Italian word that applies. The campanilista, or bell-tower-ist, is the local character who drones on, putting visitors to sleep with rich extra helpings of touristic information and meaningless lore. As Representative Pallone understood, the town's distinction embodies an ethnic, immigrant-family regard for history, a nervy alternative to the Daughters of the American Revolution.

The actor James O'Neill, father of playwright Eugene, built his oceanfront house in North Long Branch with money he made by playing the Count of Monte Cristo thousands of times. The celebrity gambler Diamond Jim Brady came to town with his girlfriend the stage star Lillian Russell. At dusk, Brady and Russell rode along the oceanfront in one of the early electric automobiles. The couple in their jewels and finery were illuminated by electric lights inside the vehicle. A fleet of spare cars and their drivers trailed behind the couple's car, in case of a breakdown or low battery. President Grant—like Brady and Russell not a figure of the old elites—raced his horses along the beach. In other words, I come from somewhere. When people assume I grew up in "the city" or "the suburbs" the campanilista in me bridles. Neither term applies.

On July 2, 1881, at the Washington train station, about to embark for a summer vacation in Long Branch, President James Garfield was shot. The president lingered for many weeks in the scorching D.C. heat. Ambitious doctors came to a White House hung with cold sheets and fans, for the distinction of poking their fingers into the poor man's wound, in search of the bullet. Alexander Graham Bell came to the bedside with an early form of metal detector. Thrown off by the metal bedsprings, Bell's device failed to detect the bullet. It was found, harmlessly encysted, after the president died of an infection, likely caused by the unwashed hands of all those eminent doctors.

The swamps of Washington were malarial. The president said he longed for the ocean breezes. On September 5, they carried him on his mattress to a special railroad car packed with ice. Overnight, dozens of men came from the town's resort hotels to help build a railroad spur from the Elberon station to the Francklyn Cottage on the ocean, where the president for a while seemed to be feeling better. But the infection returned and Garfield died on September 19.

The assassin, a screwball named Charles Julius Guiteau, had mingled with the vacationers on Long Branch's boardwalk, trying to sell copies of a book he wrote and self-published. The book's title was *The Truth*. Newspapers and even history books sometimes describe Guiteau as "a frustrated office seeker." That is whitewash. The office the assassin wanted, though he had no government experience, was ambassador to France. Guiteau had spent time at the utopian Oneida Community, which practiced a form of sexual freedom called "group marriage." Guiteau may be the only person, ever, who failed to find a sexual partner there. He was crazy, but the country wanted to punish the killer of a popular president, so Guiteau was hung on June 30, 1882, almost exactly a year after he shot Garfield at the D.C. train station.

The story of the assassination, on a larger scale than the Pinsky and Eisenberg stories, was more evidence that history, on every level, is tragic and comic, powerful and a mess. The Garfield School was my primary school. On my walk there every day I passed by the Phil Daly Hose Company, a firehouse endowed by the famous nineteenth century gambler. The name "Phil Daly" sounded like he might be a friend of my grandfather's. I may have supposed that he was. On the same walk to school, the other Rockwell kids and I also passed my father's optical office, as well as the Piano Bar, where I later played in the band, and where the Mob boss Vito Genovese presided.

Some of my campanilista information comes from a book. *Entertaining a Nation: The Career of Long Branch* was published the year I was born as part of the Writers' Project of the New Deal. Local histories, like the murals in many U.S. post offices, or footpaths in the national parks, were part of the Roosevelt administration's response to the Great Depression. The idea was that the government in a democracy takes on a role played elsewhere, in other times, by royal patrons.

When I was in the seventh grade, *Entertaining a Nation*, in battered hardcover copies, was a required textbook. The Depression-era mayor Alton Evans—his grandchild Judy Evans was my classmate—and his team wrote good sentences, and they did some impressive research. The writers were Long Branch residents Reynolds Sweetland, drama critic for the *Wall Street Journal*, and Joseph Sugarman, Jr. In *Entertaining a Nation*, they do not flinch from the story of Garfield's assassination. Even more impressively, they are not afraid to tell about the great Tri-State Ku Klux Klan gathering, attended by many thousands of Klansmen who gathered in Long Branch's Elkwood Park on July 4, 1924.

The Klan's July Fourth parade of men in pointy-headed white getups marching down Broadway seven or eight abreast, extended over a mile, from well beyond Dave Pinsky's Broadway Tavern at one end of town and past Dr. Vineberg's office at the other end, to the ocean. The procession of besheeted figures from that tri-state konklave took four hours to pass a given spot. The authors of *Entertaining a Nation* wrote:

> . . . the effect on Long Branch business was disastrous. The Jewish summer residents departed from the town the next day practically *en masse*, leaving a deserted city of ruined shopkeepers and empty hotels and boarding houses. The Negro population locked its doors tight and refused to emerge on the streets for several days. Similarly, Catholics, for whose benefit several fiery crosses had been burned, either left the community or took steps to protect themselves.

This is good writing. I like "for whose benefit" about the burning crosses, and the contrast between the French "*en masse*" and the plain English "empty hotels."

Years before I read about the konklave in *Entertaining a Nation*, I heard about it from my mother. Lethal idiocy was her kind of material, as it was for Mel Brooks, Richard Pryor and Norman Steinberg, when they wrote the script for *Blazing Saddles*. As Sylvia Pinsky told it, she recognized the shoes of one marching figure as he shuffled by, despite his white robe. She identified the brogans of Daniel "Chief" Logan, our town's high school history teacher and football coach.

That story was almost certainly her fabrication, likely based on a passage in *Entertaining a Nation* where nuns from Our Lady Star of the Sea recognize the boots of their ice-man under his Klan gown. In 1924, when the Klan marched down Broadway, Sylvia Eisenberg was seven years old and living in Arkansas or Texas, as I figured out much later. She came to Long Branch when she entered high school—a newcomer, like her enemy P. Kirk Pettiford. But from what I know about Chief Logan (not his real name), who was still teaching history when I was at Long Branch High School, her story about him did have some poetic truth. And who knows, there might have been another, smaller Klan parade in her own time.

Her conflict with Kirk Pettiford kept smoldering and erupting until one day the state of New Jersey abruptly dissolved the problem. Some lobby or other made its point and the governor signed a law that made partnership between an optometrist and an optician illegal.

Kirk remained in their office on Broadway, doing his meticulous eye-chart examinations. My father moved around the corner to a space on Third Avenue, a few doors away from the Piano Bar, haunt of the powerful crime boss. At his televised testimony before Senator Kefauver's committee investigating organized crime, Vito Genovese wore distinctive yellow lenses made by Milford S. Pinsky, Optician.

The partnership's original dark green sign stayed at the Broadway office, with "P. Kirk Pettiford, Optometrist" remaining on the right half while the left-hand side, in an unsymmetrical bit of eccentric restraint or penny-pinching—or lack of sechel, a Yiddish word sometimes translated as "savvy"—was left as a solid, dark green blank forever: a rich, and in a way poetic, aftermath.

VII

Naming Names

THINK I remember the exact moment when I became a writer. When I was nine or ten I read the Alice books over and over. I was reading them all the time, feeling what happened in them purely, innocent of much distinction between a book and a movie, between a movie and a fantasy, between playing cowboys and hearing a Tom Mix cowboy story on the radio. It was all *story*, and in that way it was all real.

In my favorite book, *Through the Looking Glass*, my favorite passage was the story of Alice and the Fawn, in the wood where things have no names. Studying the Tenniel illustration, I was moved by the awkwardness of Alice's arms clasped around the Fawn's neck as they walk together. The girl and the animal look peaceful and a little sad, as though they sense the coming moment when they will leave the wood and Alice will remember her name—she felt sure it began with an *L*— and the Fawn will cry out joyously, "I'm a Fawn!" and then, "And, dear me, you're a human child!" With a "sudden look of alarm" in its "beautiful brown eyes," the Fawn runs away.

One day I decided to give myself the pleasure of reading that story again. The illustration made the page easy to find.

But what I remembered like a feature-length movie was less than a page. It was just a few sentences I could cover with one hand! That seemed impossible, but there it was. From "Just then a Fawn came wandering by" to "it had darted away at full speed" the whole vivid episode takes only a couple of hundred words. I felt, first, a mixture of outrage and mystification. How could the book I loved trick me that way? With so few words? Then, I felt wonder. How was something so real created in such a small space? How had the writer built so much inside my mind? A kind of question I keep trying to answer.

I ALSO read and reread Mark Twain's *A Connecticut Yankee in King Arthur's Court.* That book mocked the old European pieties and hierarchies while also making them fascinating. Twain's King Arthur was a jerk, but genuinely noble. I finished the book and within a few minutes began reading it again from page one, the way I read and reread the Alice books or Robert Louis Stevenson's *Treasure Island.*

I read the novel *Ivanhoe* and saw the movie, in which order I can't remember. In Walter Scott's tale, the oppressed Saxons suffered as displaced underdogs, bravely loyal to their old nobility even though the snooty, dominant Normans treated them like dirt. As a disciple of Twain, I chose even then to refer to the writer as "Walter Scott" without the "Sir."

Ivanhoe, played by Robert Taylor (not his real name), had class. The nasty Prince John as played by Guy Rolfe did not have class, and neither did that crook the Sheriff of Nottingham, played by Basil Rathbone. Elizabeth Taylor (her real name) certainly did have class, and so did the beautiful Jewish girl Rebecca that she played in the movie *Ivanhoe.*

At the age of eleven, from the limited perspective of Long Branch in the middle of the twentieth century, in a family where I heard Yiddish every day, I pondered the attachment of Ivanhoe, the knightly Saxon, to the Jew named Isaac of Monmouth (played by British actor Felix Aylmer) and to Isaac's exquisite daughter Rebecca. Will the gentiles—good, bad and indifferent ones—kill her, or marry her, or what? That urgent question somehow involved three kinds of name: the fictional names of characters, the real or made-up names of actors, and the names of us real people.

Cultural information like the significance of names gets inhaled from no particular source, at no particular moment. As a child I somehow knew already that the names Scott, Evans, Rathbone, Stevenson, Roberts, Rolfe, Taylor and Aylmer were different from Pinsky in a fundamental way.

I puzzled over the name Isaac of Monmouth. Not Goldberg or Shapiro (or Pinsky) but "of Monmouth." Long Branch is in Monmouth County. I lived near Monmouth Avenue. It was as though Walter Scott had anticipated the name changes to place names, far in the future, of many American Jews. From some twisting, invisible grapevine, I knew the last names Berlin and London were Jewish. More precisely, they were Jewish substitutes for previous names. So why not Monmouth? Or was that pattern misleading, was Isaac of Monmouth's name not a product of anglicizing?—a word I hadn't learned yet for something I already knew.

The name changes I mean include not just the obvious Stein to Stone or Levitch to Lewis but, for example, the name of Willis Barnstone, a distinguished poet and translator. Willis's father had transformed the family name, changing its aura drastically, by shifting a couple of vowels. Bernstein to Barnstone. In the magical sounds of words, that slight a change can transform the feeling from a lower Manhattan deli to a Northumberland farmstead. In my own family, I have many Penn cousins, some of them Asians. Their name was created when my father's brother Morton Pinsky, my uncle Bunny, became Martin Penn.

The main screenwriter for that 1952 *Ivanhoe*, Marguerite Roberts, was blacklisted in Hollywood after she defied the House Un-American Activities Committee. To the shame of MGM and the Screen Writers Guild, her name—she was born with it, in Nebraska—was removed from the movie's credits. For nine years, she could not work as a screenwriter.

In the movie Marguerite Roberts wrote, the beautiful Jewess Rebecca of Monmouth is condemned to burn at the stake by the fanatical Christian order of Knights Templar. Rescued from burning by Ivanhoe, Rebecca is Elizabeth Taylor at the height of her radiance. As a clumsy Norman warrior, the hefty character actor who portrays a man falling love with Rebecca against his will could recognize that she was something special. So could an eleven-year-old boy.

In that movie, the social qualities of good looks, good speech and good manners were ideals that seemed to come along with physical courage. All were contrasted, more or less explicitly, with a different social fact: the spurious but real power of high birth. For me, as for Twain's Connecticut Yankee—and for Marguerite Roberts, I imagine—those ancient British conflicts felt like they were struggling toward some kind of American, democratic idea.

In 1960, eight years after the movie of *Ivanhoe* and its disgraceful suppression of screenwriter credit for Marguerite Roberts, she was able to strike back against the blacklisters, with her screenplay for *Spartacus*, based on a left-wing historical novel by Howard Fast. The movie was produced by its star, Kirk Douglas (the former Issur Danielovich). In the movie's most famous scene, multiple rebel slaves each say to the menacing authorities, "*I* am Spartacus." Roberts saw to it that the movie gave explicit credit, by his real name, to her colleague the blacklisted screenwriter Dalton Trumbo.

The Roman slaves of *Spartacus*, the Saxons of *Ivanhoe*, the Connecticut Yankee of Twain's novel all reflect the myth of the resourceful youngest child or scorned outsider who triumphs against the odds, like Joseph in the Hebrew Bible. Joseph was a skillful interpreter of dreams, as my already-evolving literary mind noticed. That element of dreams and their imaginative interpretation more than compensated for the fact that unlike Joseph I was not a youngest child but the oldest of three. I felt free to make my own choices and edits among stories and their versions.

Somewhere I had heard or read that in the original French story Cinderella's slipper was made of fur—transformed into glass by a mistaken translation into English. "Verre" and "vair" (old word for fur) had been confused. But no—that interesting, quasi-scholarly information is not true, but just an urban legend I believed for years. It remains a good example of how, in matters of language, a happy mistake might be superior to literal correctness. The extra fold of mistake makes the story better. Glass as a mis-translation of fur, made-up, folklore about folklore—and what isn't? The kind of writing I love would be nowhere without similar contraptions, momentary cons and improvised memories.

With luck, provincial naïfs and undaunted immigrants could absorb the best of the old, inherited orders and exceed them. So I was led to believe by the story of Joseph, and by the movies, and by Mark Twain, by all sorts of jokes and family stories, and even by comic strip adventures—not just *Superman* but *Terry and the Pirates* and my favorite, *Captain Easy*, probably still a model for me with its blend of risky adventure and comedy.

The immigrant moguls who created the movie industry understood money in relation to language in general, and to names in particular. They renamed Spangler Brugh so he became Robert Taylor, eligible to portray the Saxon underdog Ivanhoe. Watching the movie, I listened intensely to the former Brugh as Ivanhoe and Elizabeth Taylor as Rebecca and Felix Aylmer as Isaac of Monmouth as they spoke lines I couldn't know were written by the blacklisted Marguerite Roberts.

I did not know (or care) that those words she wrote, spoken by the actors, were different from the prose of Walter Scott. Later, as a reader I began to hear how unlike speech Scott's clunky prose is, compared to the vocal dash of *Treasure Island*. In that book Stevenson's writing fit with the idea that speaking is the highest form of breathing.

Names matter to American immigrants, and maybe to Jews in particular. Quite different from skin tone or bank accounts but, like those other social barometers, names inspire scrutiny and anxiety. (I can think immediately of three or four jokes on the subject.) How, and how much, did I notice, beginning at what age, that the two movie stars of *Ivanhoe*, Elizabeth and Robert, had the same last name? Did spelling Taylor with a *y* elevate the name to make it classier than Tailor: a trade in the garment industry, that immigrant gateway?

Now, toward the other end of my life, names come to mind again, each name also a word, with its meanings. And the combination of first with last name is a phrase, as in "Elizabeth Taylor" or "Felix Aylmer" with their social connotations and implications. Alice embraces the Fawn and they walk together in an Eden without names, or where names are not rational or social realities, but purely vocal and internal, a realm where "Alice" does begin with an *L*. As Alice and the Fawn leave that paradise without names, the definitions come back, and they part.

After midnight on March 13, 2020, a young emergency medical technician was shot dead, in her Lexington, Kentucky, apartment, by police officers who had battered down her door. There is no evidence that she or her apartment had anything to do with any crime. She was a Black woman and her name was Taylor. Breonna Taylor's killing was not prosecuted as a murder. My personal experiences of history, in all senses of that word, lead me to consider how the prosecutors, or the judge who issued a warrant to invade her apartment, read meaning in the two words "Breonna Taylor."

Milford Pinsky's unusual first name is a variation on the names of English poets—Milton, Herbert, Sidney—that immigrants in his parents' generation chose for their children. Early in my life I recognized a live, irrational creature that was dreadful and fascinating. It was culture itself. It made him Milford and it made her Breonna. The world, with its ways. The consequences of names or skins are among its tentacles and plumes.

I knew that if the five of us in my family stood next to our across-the-street neighbor the Black doctor J. C. McKelvie and his family, or from around the corner on Monmouth Avenue the Hanfords and the Weavers, then the color of our skin alone, with no other evidence, would establish a higher standing for us. As a young child I had learned, somehow, that the difference protected us from violence, including police brutality, even death.

Beyond a doubt, even my enemies in authority, the teachers who didn't like my wise-guy attitude or my looks or my name, were ready to treat Billy Hanford and Lloyd Weaver in ways far more damaging than any injustice or prejudice—to use the old word—that they would inflict on me. As children, both Judy Talcott and I had large vocabularies for our age. I knew Judy even before we were in kindergarten together at the Garfield School. We graduated from high school together. Under the taken-for-granted, pathological rule of white supremacy, that early knack with words would eventually be more to my benefit than hers. That was true even though Judy's last name, compared to mine, was more like the names of movie heroes, politicians and historical figures. My skin was more like theirs. These are facts I could perceive pretty early, but was capable of understanding only in confusion, on my own. Maybe I could have understood better or sooner, with more help? Possibly so, which is cause to rejoice that many American schools now assign writing by Toni Morrison and Frederick Douglass.

I also knew, again without understanding, that if all of those family names appeared in a list, with no other evidence, then Talcott, Hanford, Weaver (in the second house around the corner of Rockwell and Monmouth) and McKelvie would be a much better asset than Pinsky. Those names, unlike Pinsky, suggest the dominant, majority religion of the United States. Not nearly an equivalent of race—in a different league of vulnerability—but another example of actual, governing realities and codes that are all the more fearsome for being insane.

By my early teens or before, I had a rudimentary understanding that the Protestant-sounding names of Black people had a nightmare history in slavery. Skin color had an incomparably more awful American meaning than did the sound of names. But the two, skin and names, had been welded together. Years later, Muhammad Ali was teaching the world about what he meant by "slave names." In my spotty but sometimes intense need to learn things, especially things about words and speech, I read much later about the original Cassius Clay, who was a white emancipationist from a slave-owning family. I felt the need to understand, and also the more peculiar need—a kind of quirk—to include in the effort all of my own uncertainty and confusion. My ignorance itself began to interest me. Confusion could be a more interesting subject than purity.

It interests me that only a few years ago did I learn a civic fact about names and the Holocaust: that a first step of the Nazi bureaucracy was to deprive German Jews of first names, such as "Kurt" or "Anna," that might have been in their family for generations. On all legal documents, all Jewish men were by law re-named "Israel" and all women "Sarah," with the former, non-Jewish first names possibly to follow parenthetically as in a footnote, for clarity.

As the wheel turned, Jeff Goldblum could remain Jeff Goldblum and Dante Smith could become Mos Def and Mos Def could become Yasiin Bey. Malcolm X, who had been Detroit Red and became el-Hajj Malik el-Shabazz, demonstrated forever the boundless importance of American names. About the time Jews began to stop changing their names as a prudent disguise, Black Americans began asserting African or Islamic surnames as the opposite of disguise.

One faction says the only truly Jewish names are Levine and Cohen. But like other nominally Orthodox Jews, I have a Hebrew name. Within a synagogue, I am Ruveyn Nachman ben Moshe. On my birth certificate, "Robert Neal" (the middle name I never use) is a secular, outward, phonetic equivalent based on the Hebrew initial letters. "Pinsky" in this context is a sort of colonial afterthought, adopted a few generations back, for use on official documents—taxes, immigration. About Jewish names in the English language, my poker friend Bernie Katz taught me that his surname is a scholarly acrostic for "tzadikkim cohenim": the Wise among the Priests. (I had associated the name with cats.) I never think of myself as "Ruveyn," but there it is.

Generations earlier, an immigrant Polish Jew called Goldwasser changed his name, which on a document in his native Poland signified, "NOT ONE OF US POLES." He wandered to Arizona, and in two or three generations his descendants could evolve (or devolve?) to produce the Episcopalian cowboy Barry Goldwater, a conservative Republican candidate for president. That extreme case of fluidity, for my family in New Jersey, inspired both satire and a cynical kind of admiration.

The traditional fluidity (not so available to the Weavers, Hanfords, Talcotts and McKelvies, needless to say) has a nice reversal, in Vince Gilligan's *Breaking Bad* and *Better Call Saul*. In those television dramas, the sleazy attorney Jimmy McGill changes his name to Saul Goodman, the better to market himself as a Jewish lawyer. That reverse name change would amuse my parents the way they were amused by Kirk Pettiford's sign. Nightmares are complicated, and they involve desires.

VIII

Ironfoot, Ruveyn and Folkenflik

I T TOOK me years to understand that this habit of thinking about names was essential to my work as a poet.

I think I always knew or guessed that the first name of my father's partner Kirk Pettiford meant "church." My assumption about the family name "Pettiford" was that it meant a small ford, for crossing a river. But more interesting than that, a bit of Web research indicates that the name comes from the Old French word "pedefer," or "pied de fer," which means iron foot. Pedefer might be a nickname for a patient, sturdy walker: Iron Foot. Or the name might designate a soldier who lost a foot in battle. In either meaning, Kirk Pettiford's name is an unexpected example of anglicizing. Norman French meanings that lurked inside what I had thought of as Middle American. The mills of time and place invisibly grinding and mixing and remaking, forever—a workplace for poetry.

"Pinsky" comes from a place, Pinsk—mostly Jewish, and the population mostly exterminated by the Nazis. In my Berkeley years, Czesław Miłosz describe Pinsk for me as he remembered it. He told me I mispronounced it. "Peensk" had a river, a sawmill. But where I grew up, "Pinsky" with a short *i* was a local name. Dave Pinsky's bar, the Broadway Tavern, was across the street from the city hall and the police station. The cops and politicians drank there, and in July, when the horses were running at Monmouth Park, so did many jockeys, trainers and bookies. Lots of people were customers of both the Broadway Tavern and Milford S. Pinsky, Optician. If I had a run-in with anybody, one of my father's first questions would be sort of Homeric:

"Did they know who you are?"

When I was twelve years old, I saw my father's friend and customer Leroy Folkenflik artfully deploy a classic name joke, one of the oldest. Leroy was a veteran of the war in Korea, with a Purple Heart and a wooden leg he enjoyed rapping with his knuckles for the proverbial "knock wood." In a wholesale or subcontractor arrangement, my father made eyeglasses in batches for Leroy and for the ophthalmologist Merritt Evan London, M.D.

Dr. London was fair-haired, blue-eyed, and a foot taller than Leroy Folkenflik. One day when I was helping out in my father's office I listened as Dr. London confided to Leroy that yes, his father had changed the family name to London from Lowenstein.

"It's a practical thing, changing the name, and I'm glad my father did it. Have you ever thought of changing yours?"

Leroy had plenty of experience being a Folkenflik in settings such as grade school and the United States Army. The name, like the wooden leg, was something he liked to joke about. He answered Dr. London with an ancient move, adeptly timed.

"Well," Leroy said to Dr. London, "my brother Myron changed his name. He got tired of being Myron Folkenflik."

"Oh, that's interesting. What did he change it to?"

"Sidney Folkenflik."

Leroy Folkenflik's exchange with Merritt Evan London

was a miniature version of the story told by *Ivanhoe* or *Sparta-cus*, the triumph of a gifted underdog who defends the author-ity of a surviving past.

I wasn't surprised when I read—for one example among so many—that the painter Philp Guston was born Philip Gold-stein. Retaining "Philip" as his first name could be regarded as, in effect, a loyal, secular and cosmopolitan challenge to the Nazi bureaucracy that would have designated him as "Israel"—or, in a way, "Ruveyn."

After I moved to Berkeley, California, I learned a different perspective. For my kids in their teens, my New Jersey ear for names and ethnicities seemed not just obsolete but a bit offensive. In their generation and in that place, a lot of the ethnic nuance I've tried to describe here was rude nonsense. If I told them to go to the Armenian tailor, or to ask for the Italian guy named Gary at the car repair place, they'd scold me a little.

"Dad, you're kind of racist. What difference does it make if he's Armenian or Italian?"

Of course, I loved my children's apparent deafness to the historical distinctions I couldn't help hearing among, say, Leary, Suarez, Iqbal, Cohen, Jackson and Chang. In the social set of Nicole, the oldest, there was an unusually hand-some kid who was called Guapo Chang. Berkeley was far from exempt from the American binary racial divide, or other vicious delusions about names, religions, ancestry. But in Cal-ifornia the infection had taken different forms from those of New Jersey fifty years earlier.

A fellow Jewish throwback from the East was my Berke-ley colleague Leonard Michaels, the brilliant fiction writer. Lenny and his family lived in Kensington, an unincorporated area above the Berkeley Hills. Lenny grew up in a New York tenement with Yiddish as his first language. He asked me for a favor. He wanted his son Jesse to attend middle school in the city of Berkeley, where I had just come to live. So Lenny and I went to an office where we filled out forms declaring that Jesse Michaels was my nephew, and he would be living with me at 1924 Monterey Avenue, Berkeley 94707. The false claim worked, and Jesse attended middle school in Berkeley. He later became a celebrated songwriter in genres like "second wave ska punk."

At an English Department dinner party one evening not long after Lenny and I submitted those forms, someone at the table asked me if what they heard could possibly be true. I was new to Berkeley, having taken the job there quite recently.

"Robert, did you really sign your name to a false document, for Lenny Michaels?"

The question brought up my past in a challenging way different from the world of my children and Guapo Chang. How could I do such a thing? the dinner party guests wanted to know. It was illegal. Did I really make a false claim on an official government form? What if that fact came out?

These were good questions, and I had not considered them. Asking myself why that was so, at the table with my new Berkeley colleagues and their spouses, I thought about Long Branch, my parents and their friends. Possibly I thought about my grandfather in the liquor business during Prohibition, and his friends. In that world, you put personal relationships above rules, when you could. You might not—don't be a fool!—but if possible, you went with loyalty over truth. A fib in the interest of where a child went to school would be a respected example.

So, at that Berkeley dinner party I spoke an unintended laugh line:

"I guess it all depends," I said, "on how you were brought up."

* * *

THAT GATHERING of Yale and Harvard Ph.D.s. at the dinner party seemed to think I was being witty. Their laughter was not cruel. But if they assumed I was confessing to a bad upbringing, they were wrong. In a sense, I did that favor for Lenny Michaels to uphold the honor of the Pinsky family name.

I remember another moment involving Lenny and names. I had sent my poem "The Figured Wheel" to *The New Yorker*, and the editor Howard Moss wrote me a kindly note saying that they liked the poem quite a lot, but could I please edit a line toward the end so it would no longer include my name. In what became the title poem of my 1996 volume of new and collected poems, the figured wheel rolls over many things, and in the concluding lines it rolls over "the haunts of Robert Pinsky's mother and father / And wife and children and his sweet self / Which he hereby unwillingly and inexpertly gives up, because it is // There, figured and pre-figured in the nothing transfiguring wheel."

An important, freeing moment for me as a writer came when I rebelled against the academic notion of attributing a poem's words always to "the speaker," not the poet. The request that I edit out my name reminded me how and why I liked breaking the conventional, assumed separation between the author's name, in a credit or byline for the poem, and what is in the poem. As though all poems were automatically dramatic. I liked ignoring that rule. For a long time I had wanted to emulate the seventeenth century poet Ben Jonson, who used his own name in a couple of great poems.

But this was *The New Yorker* back in the days when it did not print the words "fuck" and "shit." The magazine was excellent and it was also decorous. For many years it had no contents page; the authors' names appeared only at the ends of articles. Possibly that old, genteel discretion about names heightened my commitment to my name staying in "The Figured Wheel."

Anyway, politely refusing to delete the words "Robert Pinsky," I declined Howard Moss's offer to publish the poem.

When Lenny Michaels, a practical man, heard about that decision, he told me I was crazy.

"Who cares about your literary principles?" Lenny said. "You should let them publish the fucking poem, and then write another one."

IX

Brave, Clean and Reverent

DON'T MEAN to exaggerate. Life in Long Branch was ordinary. It was not a lowlife TV show or a gangster series or movie. But at the top of the gangster genre, the very title *The Godfather* expresses a social idea I recognize. A relationship that is not blood can be like blood.

And sometimes a social relationship, with its quasi-religious demands and its ranks and rituals, can be even more intense than blood ties. The Puzo-Coppola story begins with what resembles a royal wedding, with an emphasis not just on splendor and celebration but also on petitioners: high and low, with their needs attended to by the patriarch, who is shown in a regal position to favor and appreciate each petitioner in ways greater than they can appreciate or benefit him in return. As with other forms of patronage, the arrangement is corrupt and practical, in ways that vary with different people.

When Milford Pinsky was composing his definition of a gentleman, he and his sister Thelma lived with their father Dave Pinsky in an apartment above his bar, the Broadway Tavern. Across the street were the city hall and the police department. Here is a story from the *Newark Evening News* of August 22, 1929, telling about David Pinsky's role in organized crime. This was about five years before the Monmouth professor accused Dave's firstborn son Milford of academic dishonesty. The headline was "Indicts Twelve in Big Liquor Plot at Shore, U.S. Jury Acts on Five Plants at Long Branch, Shrewsbury, Cliffwood":

> One of the largest liquor conspiracy cases in New Jersey prohibition history was disclosed when the Federal Grand Jury returned six indictments yesterday afternoon against twelve men charged with operating five large distilling plants in Long Branch, Shrewsbury and Cliffwood . . . Three plants were operated in Long Branch, it is charged, with stills up to 1,000 gallons capacity . . . The distilling equipment was valued at several hundred thousand dollars.

And under the subhead "Six Are Arrested":

> Among the twelve men under indictment are Morris and Isidore Schneider, David Pinsky, Joseph Bender, Joseph Tomaini and Charles Petti, all of Long Branch.

Three stills, each producing a thousand gallons per day. So much for my mother's wisecracks about her husband's family making gin in the bathtub. "Several hundred thousand dollars" must be the 1929 equivalent of four or five million today.

I once asked my uncle Bunny, my father's younger brother, "If your father was in the Mob, selling liquor, how come we aren't rich?"

"They gave him his choice," said Bunny.

The situation was a bit like Izzy Ash's junkyard story of Barry Green, the lawyer who went to prison over a Mob-soaked deal involving orange peels and synthetic sugar. The newspaper story implies that Dave Pinsky, his friend Joe Tomaini and the others were not big bosses:

> The indictments were handed to the court along with a presentment in which the grand jury urged the prohibition authorities to get the principals in liquor cases rather than the underlings.

As underlings, Pinsky, Schneider, Petti, Bender and Tomaini had two possibilities, according to my uncle. One was to get paid, go to prison and keep silent. The other was don't get paid, keep silent and stay out of prison. In my opinion, Zaydee Pop made the right choice. Instead of prison time and a bundle, he got his freedom and the Broadway Tavern.

When those indictments came down, my father was twelve years old—a likely age for craving respectability and other attributes of a gentleman. The language of the newspaper story, with its legalese like "presentment" and the contrasting blunt "underlings"—tweezers and a wrench—has an old-time charm I can enjoy from a distance. From up close, the same words might have been humiliating, even terrifying.

Respectability might have had a romantic, even exotic aura for young Milford and Thelma, for reasons beyond their father's arrest. Their mother, Rose Schacter Pinsky, was said to be a famous beauty, as confirmed by old photographs. One of them, her portrait in an oval frame, is on the headstone of Rose's grave, preserved by an impressive sealed-glass technology of those days. The elaborate headstone is in the shape of a tree with its branches lopped off, to represent a life that ended too soon.

Rose died in her twenties, leaving Dave with Sonny (my father), who was six years old, and Babe (my aunt Thelma), who was four. She lived only a few days after giving birth to her third child, my aunt Evelyn (Toots). The young mother never came home from the hospital. Dave Pinsky went after the doctor with a pistol. The story is that his business partner and fellow underling Joe Tomaini rushed after him to the hospital, where he took away the gun and convinced Dave that for his children's sake he needed to spare the doctor.

But the young gangster Dave, after he had expressed his grief with that extravagant headstone, and by threatening to shoot the doctor, still had a family. One of Dave's sisters and her husband adopted the infant Evelyn (Toots), who grew up as Evelyn Kassoff. He now needed someone to help him care for his two small children Milford and Thelma. (Or, as everyone called them, Sonny and Babe.) Rose's family, Dave's in-laws the Schacters, filled that need by supplying Dave with a new wife: Rose's cousin Molly.

It was Molly's unhappy mission to care for Dave and his kids as a substitute for Rose, the great love of his life, the beauty with her memorial picture set onto the marble tree with severed branches. Poor Molly, as I often heard her described. Life was not easy for her as the young gangster's second wife, assigned to keep house and to raise little Thelma and Milford. But Dave gave Molly two more babies, Dorothy and Morton.

Those words, that Dave "gave her two more babies," were something I heard my father say, in anger. He used it one day toward the end of his life when I watched him arguing with his sister Thelma—Sonny and Babe both in their eighties but still at it, debating their father's conduct. Witnessing their argument made me feel something like the detached fascination of a child, which can be mistaken for innocence. I was a child watching the anger of two children. I seemed to be invisible to them.

"Sonny," she said, "that's life. It was rotten for everybody. You can't really blame him."

"I can too," he said. "I do blame him, Babe. It was wrong, and you know it."

"But Sonny, what do you expect? So he didn't love Molly. All right. But he was a young man, they gave him Molly to be his wife, and there she was—a young woman, right there. No beauty, but a young woman, his wife! What do you expect? Then Della came to work in the bar. She gave him something Molly couldn't. Poor Molly. It wasn't nice for her—but there it is."

"He shouldn't have given her the two more babies!"

Overhearing this conversation helped me understand the family history I couldn't untangle as a child. But I had already understood the voices and faces. My father and my aunt were mad at their father in different ways. They were not rejecting their sister and brother Dot and Bunny, Molly's children with Dave. The intimacy of the nicknames were at the heart of the argument. They were all family, Toots included, and in their guts and their voices they all knew one another in ways nobody else could. I was in an outer ring of that knowing.

I never heard my aunts and uncles refer to one another as "half brother" or "half sister." Those are terms our family didn't use, maybe because the "half" would have brought up some submerged shame, but more than that, they were bonded together against the respectable world. In the patriarchal setup, they were all Dave's children, Sonny, Babe, Toots, Dot and Bunny, brothers and sisters. Even Toots, taken away as an infant a few days after her mother died, to be a Kassoff— she was Dave's child and their sister, period.

As kids do, I accepted confusing family ways. I knew that my first cousin Leslie, my aunt Evelyn's son, called Anna and Izzie Kassoff "Grandma" and "Grandpa" and I called them "Aunt Anna" and "Uncle Izzy." I knew that Aunt Anna was the sister of Dave Pinsky, Cousin Leslie's grandfather and mine. Aunt Anna was somehow Leslie's grandma. His grandpa was my grand-uncle. A mix-up not interesting enough for us kids to pay much attention.

The family bonded together, but as children they came

to be physically separate: Toots, Cousin Leslie's mother, was in North Jersey with the Kassoffs. In Long Branch, after Dave left Molly, Sonny and Babe were living above the bar with their father and the barmaid, Dave's girlfriend Della Sawyer. And a few blocks away, Dot and Bunny lived with their mother Molly in rooms behind Perry's Bowling Center: Dave's second household.

Not long ago, my sweet, understated aunt Dot told me in a matter-of-fact way that Dave was neglectful toward that second family, and toward her mother poor Molly. When the heat was cut off from their apartment behind Perry's, she told me, it was her brother Sonny who brought them extra blankets from the apartment above the Broadway Tavern. Aunt Dot also told me that the only one who came to her mother's funeral—she was a little girl herself, hadn't known why she was wearing a new dress—was Sonny, my father.

After Molly was sent to the state mental hospital at Marlboro for the last time, her children, too, finally moved into Dave's apartment above the bar, with Dot and Bunny living as one family with their father and Sonny and Thelma and Della, the barmaid.

My mother always spoke of Della as "the Barmaid," the way she liked to call her father-in-law Dave a moonshiner or a bootlegger. The nouns were another way to tease her husband. Sometimes he tried to fight back, maybe by noting that Sylvia was repeating her material. It was all theater, and I was an audience. She might succeed in getting him angry, or they might start having fun, laughing together at his pedantic explanation.

"Sylvia, you have it wrong. See, the moonshiners *make* it and it's the bootleggers that move it around and *sell* it."

I remember Della Sawyer as a scary lady with a lot of rouge on her face. When I was growing up, she and Dave still lived above the Broadway Tavern, a few blocks away from Long

Branch High School, where all of us graduated. I walked past the bar every day on my way to school, where I might sit in that same classroom where Milford Pinsky took his aborted night school course in English Composition.

Della became, more or less, the mother of all five of Dave's kids after Molly went to Marlboro. The name Marlboro has an odor of dread and shame, still, for anybody who remembers it: Marlboro, the state mental institution of New Jersey. Molly was sent there, and returned home for a time, and was sent back to Marlboro again and died there, possibly a suicide.

Molly too is buried in the Long Branch cemetery, the records show, along with her cousin the first wife Rose and Rose's replacement the barmaid Della Sawyer. Not far from Rose's stone tree with the lopped-off branches is Della's plainer headstone. On it, her name is inscribed as "Della Sawyer"—maybe because she and Dave never actually married, and maybe because the Sawyers, those Presbyterians, chose to avoid the Jewish "Pinsky." Names, again. And the tormented Molly has no formal grave or marker.

Molly's son, my uncle Bunny, told me that when he was growing up he felt equally rejected as an outsider by the Jewish synagogue and by the Sawyers' church. Eventually, climbing the ladder in the corporate world, he changed his name to Martin Penn—which I interpret as a rejection not of his father so much as of the past itself, a disavowal of the dictates and definitions of social classes, categories, tribes and in-groups. Another, agnostic variation of the provincial sense of time.

My father had a different way of separating himself from their father, or from the past. Milford became a Boy Scout, literally and in spirit. He rose to Star Scout, the next highest rank to Eagle Scout. He could recite from memory, at a machine-gun pace, the organization's Oath and its Law.

The Scout's Oath: "*On my honor I will do my best to do my*

duty to God and my country and to obey the Scout Law; to help other people at all times; to keep myself physically strong, mentally awake, and morally straight." He could also fire off the Scout's Law: "*A Scout is Trustworthy, Loyal, Helpful, Friendly, Courteous, Kind, Obedient, Cheerful, Thrifty, Brave, Clean, and Reverent.*" In his rhythmical, military-sounding delivery, the final "Brave, Clean, and Reverent" had the snap of a single unit, like *xyz*.

He wasn't naïve about those promises and adjectives—the singsong recitation of virtues, with a shy grin, seemed to convey respect for a quality not so much of profundity, maybe, as authority. These formulas were part of how the world worked. The Boy Scouts may have represented for my father an authority more reliable, more decent, and more socially approved than the three largest illegal stills in the history of New Jersey.

What if Milford Pinsky had lived long enough to see the Boy Scouts of America in financial bankruptcy caused by paying settlements for child abuse? His refuge of respectability disgraced? I imagine him disappointed but not crushed. He would be either nodding his head or shaking it left to right, gently, while murmuring one of his habitual words: "Terrible."

As to power, we had physical tokens of it—notably male—in our Rockwell Avenue apartment. Displayed on a shelf in the living room was a streamlined chrome bulldog, the hood ornament from the Mack Bulldog truck Dave Pinsky drove, hauling liquor from Canada to New Jersey for the mob boss Longie Zwillman. A bootlegger, in that careful distinction, not a moonshiner. On every closet doorknob, hanging by a leather thong, we had billy clubs of various shapes and designs, provided by Joe Purcell, the Long Branch policeman who had been Zaydee Pop's right-hand man back in those liquor-running days. The billy clubs and the chrome bulldog embodied a shady counter-authority to the chanted ideals of the Boy Scout's Oath.

When my father recited the Oath, what I can now call the Germanic word "Clean" hammered its blunt presence between the *v*'s of the two highfalutin French words "Brave" and "Reverent"—all in that weird, drill-sergeant chant. Hearing it gave me a pleasure like the train conductor's "Passengers going to Hoboken," or Sid Caesar's double-talking German or Japanese.

Ezra Pound says poetry is a centaur. That is, a thing of body and mind, in that order. If you are too cerebral to hear it, you miss the point. A busy compulsion to understand may be more common than its opposite, an unwillingness to think. Both extremes undermine pleasure, and both are often acquired in school. Like singing and dancing and playing sports, poetry is something nearly everybody enjoys when they are small. Somehow, we learn to fear or dislike such things. You have to be taught that you can't dance, for example, and until then you can. Same with poetry.

One of my repeated nervous jokes, when recognition comes my way, or a check, has been to say:

"And all of this—for *ta-da ta-da, ta-da ta-da ta-da*?"

Something like a protective superstition underlies that pretended belittlement. The wonderment is sincere. The reductive "*ta-da*" may mask something as lofty for me, and as vulnerable to scorn, as the Scout's Oath was for my father. I have in mind the superstitious expression (spelling the Yiddish as I have heard it) "kinna hora." For years, I heard that phrase on joyful occasions: the birth of a beautiful baby, a new dress or medical good news. I thought it meant "our happiness is complete." I was in my mid-twenties when I learned that the words mean something like "Go away, Evil Eye," a shield against the risk that enjoying good fortune might be punished.

To go into it a bit, the rhythm of "*ta-da*" is secondary in what we call poetry's "music." A conversation about actual music with Stan Strickland, the master saxophone player, vocalist and teacher, helped my understanding of spoken sounds.

"Everybody knows," Stan said, "that all music has three elements: rhythm, melody and harmony. But which came first? Nearly everybody says 'rhythm.' They talk about the heartbeat, about drums. But I don't think so. *Melody* is primary."

He explained, "A baby cries or laughs an expressive tune, before it can keep time. My dog sings his anger or fear or contentment, but he doesn't keep time while he does it. It's the sequence of pitches, their emotional meaning, the melody— that comes before the regular beat of rhythm, or the combined sounds of harmony."

Stan Strickland's contention that melody comes first confirmed my impatience with elaborate notation for rhythm or meter, the taxonomy of obsessive scansion, primary and secondary stresses, amphibrachs, pseudo-spondees, dactyls. I can shuffle or deal iambs and trochees, or discuss the prosodic equivalent of 4/4 time or 6/8 or exotics like 5/4. Arcane, secondary matters have their interest. But the unique, expressive sequence of pitches and quantities in each sentence and line is primary. The propulsive spoken tune of poetry is what first drew me to lines by Shakespeare or Yeats. Later, I listened to the same energy in the poetry of William Carlos Williams, Allen Ginsberg and Elizabeth Bishop, the pitches of the grammar singing through the rhythm, in the clangs and chimes of our profoundly mongrel, improvised and Bible-ridden American language.

Dave Pinsky, in a story I've heard from many Long Branch sources, once won a bet by throwing an apple clear over the downtown water tower. The noted literary scholar M. H. Abrams ("Mike" to my parents), introducing my poetry reading at Cornell, began by noting that "his grandfather was quite a local character." He mentioned the story of the apple thrown over the water tower, as well as the liquor business. I can't remember how he related those stories to my poetry. I'd like to think that physical ability was involved, somehow.

Mike Abrams didn't mention the scandal of my grandfather's two households, one at a bar and one behind a bowling alley, the arrangement well known to everybody in town. My mother told me that Della would drive by Molly's place in Dave's Packard and from the wheel thumb her nose at the poor woman. That may be another fabrication—how would Sylvia know? True or false, it represents the small-town trove of nasty stories and scandalous images.

Writing about little places on the prairie, Willa Cather refers to "the tongue, that terror of little towns." Terror. The fear of gossip, she proposes, gains a fearsome power as whispers are amplified by isolation in mean little prairie villages. In a comparable kind of isolation, a beachfront resort town contracts and turns inward on itself during the nine months insiders call the off-season. The centrifuge of winter agitates the tongues, so the bonanza of gossip might billow around a story like Dave with Rose, with Molly, with Della, the thug with his separate and overlapping households. All that, plus— or multiplied by—indictments and arrests in "one of the largest liquor conspiracy cases in New Jersey prohibition history."

That kind of attention might make a twelve-year-old boy whose mother died when he was six crave respectability— or maybe something above mere respectability, something more like what Henry James has his heroine solemnly ponder, something superior. Maybe to be equally as recognized in a community as a tough-guy father like Dave, but also with a reputation as reliable, truthful and law-abiding? Or as exemplified by the Scout's Oath, code-abiding? Brave, clean and reverent. After the generation of movie moguls and gangsters, or anyway distinct from them, there was a generation of working-class gentlefolk who shared certain plain, mostly unwritten rules, many of them broken by Dave. Many of those same rules were respected all the more by Milford, called Sonny. His straight-arrow qualities were a high-class form of rebellion against his father. And in the next generation, Milford's son seemed free to relish Dave's story, if not his behavior.

X

Idolatry

My GRANDFATHER Dave Pinsky's disregard for the practice of Judaism as a religion was so calm and perfect that he didn't seem to express his feelings about piety and rabbi-craft except implicitly, by living his profane life.

Without warning, Zaydee Pop sometimes showed up at the Rockwell Avenue apartment and announced that I would not be going to school that day. He would be taking me to New York with him, to keep him company on a business trip. My mother, his great opponent, did not put up much of a fight.

Their combative relationship came up in a question about one of my favorite old pictures, a studio photograph of Dave as a well-dressed young thug, handsome in an ape-like way, posed with his beautiful young bride, Rose. She is standing wearing a fur stole and a stylish hat. He is seated, with his right arm around her waist, her hand on his shoulder. She is smiling. He looks ready to punch somebody in the nose.

"What would he say," someone asked me about that picture, "if he knew his grandson was going to be a poet?" Dave's likely answer came to me right away:

"*I blame his mother.*"

MY TRIPS to New York with him always began with a stop at Vogel's department store on Long Branch's Broadway, a few blocks away from 36 Rockwell Avenue. "Vogel's" was the sponsor's name on some of my father's sports uniforms. At the store, Zaydee Pop and I would go directly to the shoe department, under the escalator. He always bought me a new pair of lace-up brogans. Once they were fitted, I did not take off the new shoes. In keeping with Dave Pinsky's style I wore them to New York. Into their box went the scuffed old pair, wrapped in tissue paper by the salesclerk.

With the shoebox in the backseat, Zaydee Pop and I took the hour's drive to Manhattan in his Packard, which was the same shade of gray as his fedora hat. The steering wheel was ivory. When I asked him what he would be doing in the city, he told me he wanted to look at some "fixtures," a noun with a mysterious allure. Maybe it meant something as innocent as barstools or overhead lights, or the Broadway Tavern's shuffleboard table. We always had lunch at Jack Dempsey's Restaurant. One time, I got to reach up and shake the heavyweight champion's hand. Then we ate our steaks.

His character and habits may have contributed to my confusions about Jews. In the adult world of famous people, I assumed Eartha Kitt was Jewish. She didn't seem to be Black or white Protestant or Italian. The way she sang her hit songs in French and Persian—"Uska Dara" sounded sort of Yiddish—had a kidding, none-of-the-above of exaggeration that reminded me of my family. Same with Cary Grant, who seemed to enjoy the joke of his own good looks and his unique accent. And if you tried to tell me Charlie Chaplin was not Jewish, I would think you were lying. He too resembled us. All of these show business figures in their different ways had an improvised, worldly quality I thought I recognized.

Dave Pinsky's ways are captured by the words of Isaiah 2, "they please themselves in the children of strangers," and "they worship the work of their own hands, that which their own fingers have made." His soul was given to the attractions of the world, the world of the senses, the world made by mortal man. Isaiah 2 concludes, with magnificent curtness, "Cease ye from man, whose breath is in his nostrils: For wherein is he to be accounted of?"

That severe biblical judgment goes beyond mere asceticism or self-denial; it condemns the adoration of all that can be made and enjoyed by the human body, with breath in its nostrils. My Zaydee Pop was an idolator. I loved Christmas at his house, with presents from my aunts and uncles and his enormous Christmas tree. Because of my mother's family, we were Orthodox. On Rockwell Avenue, next door to a boardinghouse for housepainters and pizza cooks, we kept kosher. We belonged to the Orthodox synagogue, where I was taught to chant by rote the Hebrew sounds of my haftorah, the weekly portion from the Books of the Prophets a boy was to chant on the Sabbath of his bar mitzvah. The bat mitzvah for girls had not reached our shul.

The haftorah I sang was a special one, timed for the conjunction that October of the Sabbath and the New Moon. It is the exalted, punitive concluding chapter of Isaiah, as I learned years later. This chapter assigned to me by the calendar is all the more terrifying because the words and images are supremely beautiful. I learned none of that. In the customary way, with its demanding focus on chanting the melody and mastering the Hebrew pronunciation, nobody told me that the passages I memorized and sang came from the book of the prophet Isaiah, nor what the words meant. In the social context of those immigrant elders trying to preserve what they treasured, meaning was a deferred luxury.

Learning the sounds was hard work. Laboriously through the hot summer of preparation I chanted after the teacher's voice, phrase by phonetic phrase. "Kay aumar adashem, hashawmayim keesee, es bawnehaw." In my first encounter with great poetry, I was unaware, as though "blind" to it—though to be precise I was not quite deaf to it. I heard the sounds, and I sang them. Certain moments of the tune that I learned were bluesy, in the way of Gershwin's "It Ain't Necessarily So." The only part of the words I didn't know was their meaning. Hebrew school does not use the language of the King James translation, in which my haftorah (I know now) begins:

> *Thus saith the Lord, The Heaven is my throne, and the earth is my footstool: Where is the house that ye build unto me? and where is the place of my rest?*

"If I have made everything you see," God seems to ask, in the text I chanted as a series of uncomprehended sounds, "then where in the world of the senses could you dare have the nerve to build a place for Me? Architecture is futile. Only humility, an obedient, fearful spirit apt for contrition, will prevail."

Moreover, worship itself may fail. Struggling all summer to learn the difficult performance scheduled for October, I was now and then curious (or bored) enough to peek at the facing-page translation of the Hebrew into stilted English. But I didn't peek enough to understand that I was singing an angry denunciation of hollow worship and merely outward forms of religion. In the King James translation, the next verse reads:

> *He that killeth an ox is as if he slew a man; he that sacrificeth a lamb, as if he cut off a dog's neck; he that offereth an oblation,*

as if he offered swine's blood; he that burneth incense, as if he
blessed an idol. Yea, they have chosen their own ways, and their
soul delighteth in their abominations.

—Isaiah, 66:3

Autocratic; ardent and monolithic; specific and categorical, this is the voice of Spirit, speaking here in fiery cadences of the English language. All forms of worship and ritual uninformed by the Spirit, says the voice of that Spirit itself, amount to idolatry.

Idolatry against idolatry: in the shul as my ignorant piping of Isaiah's angry denunciation of "their own ways" and in the world outside the shul those ways as practiced by my grandfather in the Broadway Tavern. If Grandpa Dave represented the allure of the secular world, his adversary was not God, and certainly was not my mother's father, my mild zaydee (without the "Pop") Morris Eisenberg. Dave's opposing force was that prophetic voice, a voice mighty even in bad translation, and commanding in the sounds of Hebrew. As I soon turned toward the larger, secular world, I heard something like that voice again in another form, clearer and more demanding than ever, in Milton, Blake and Whitman.

Isaiah denounces the sexy, sensual world in detail. Along with the degeneracy of empty, outward worship, Isaiah chides the haughty daughters of Zion, who "walk with stretched forth necks and wanton eyes, walking and mincing as they go, and making a tinkling with their feet." Their chains, bracelets, mufflers, bonnets, leg ornaments, headbands, earrings, crisping pins, wimples, hoods, fine linen, stomachers will be punished, in commensurate detail, with scabs, denuded private parts, baldness, burning rashes, and stinks.

These images show why the Israeli novelist Aharon Appelfeld, as a visiting professor at Boston University, made his required text for creative writing the Hebrew Bible. Aharon said all the modern English translations were bloodless, with abstractions like "spirit" not true to the earthy Hebrew original, where "ruach" is the word for a draft of cold or warm air, or a current in water.

"Your new moons and your appointed feasts my soul hateth; they are a trouble unto me; I am weary to bear them." Singing the memorized words of this denunciation, in a language I knew only phonetically, I was committing a kind of idolatry, less attractive and more tiring—to me as well as to God—than the kind practiced by the tinkling daughters of Zion and by their spiritual descendant Dave Pinsky. The book of Isaiah is a great poem of the void between practice and spirit. Maybe I dimly sensed that.

Chanting a condemnation of hollow worship without understanding the words: The irony is too obvious. It would be ridiculous, even heartless, to blame me at the age of twelve, cruel to blame the old men who ran the small-town synagogue, for the hypocrisy denounced by Isaiah. Those elders were immigrants without much money or knowledge of the world or education. Some had been in concentration camps. Doubtless, many of them were themselves not very comfortable with the Hebrew language. The tongue they felt at home in was Yiddish.

Mr. Gewirtz, the kind man these elders paid to teach me, was laboring uphill against the worldly forces that had entered me, the tinkling ornaments, the work of human hands, "that which their fingers have made," the pleasures created by "the children of strangers." Baseball was in the decade of Jackie Robinson and Mickey Mantle. Chuck Berry and Elvis Presley were new. Ella Fitzgerald was in her prime.

Services in the sandstone and terra-cotta shul on Second Avenue in Long Branch went from nine o'clock to sometime after noon on Saturday mornings. In other words, the sweetest hours of the week were consumed by a long, incomprehensible service in a language I didn't know, in the company of old men. The ocean was two blocks away. Outside, shadows grew shorter in the sun. Italian girls in pastel Communion dresses came to Our Lady Star of the Sea across the street, and went. Eventually, the poetry of Isaiah itself became part of that world outside the shul for me. The radiance of Isaiah's images came to resemble the profane gewgaws worn by the daughters of Zion, with the poetry of the words themselves a bodily presence, an equivalent in art of those leg ornaments and crisping pins, the veils and the wanton eyes.

The bima, or podium, of that Orthodox shul, and the ark behind it, holding the curtained Torahs in their velvet and silver fittings, were of pale oak. So too were the pews and the upstairs gallery for women. There were stained-glass windows, and a terra-cotta, Moorish-style façade. But with one exception the place lacked the theatrical Italian drama of Catholic churches I had attended a few times with friends. The light of Jewish observance was all the more passionate, retained its own spiritual meaning, for being relatively without color.

The one exception was cantorial singing, its mournful beauty embodied by a series of chazens the congregation hired, sometimes for the High Holy Days but also, on occasion, for one Sabbath. These singers were auditioning, even we bar mitzvah boys knew. The synagogue's goal was to find a permanent chazen. Sometimes a man came to Long Branch for a few months, until a better position turned up, or he was let go for some defect of character or terrible habit, no matter how splendid his voice.

The cantors sang like angels, and they carried themselves with the neurotic pride of sickly bullfighters. Those chazens, religion aside, voiced the courtship between sorrow and beauty. Though the congregation liked to criticize and compare them, even the least of the auditioning cantors could bring tears to our eyes.

The old men, the synagogue regulars, imitated the chazens, praying according to Jewish Orthodox custom aloud but not in unison, a flamboyant howling and muttering, the cantorial dandyism of various parts of Europe aped and distorted. Near the end of the three-hour service, they let themselves go wild in an orgy of competing trills, flourishes, barks and whimpers. Then they crowded the stairs to the basement, where they pressed and pushed around the post-service Sabbath feast of pickled herring, bread, sponge cake, chickpeas from a can, and the Seagram's 7 whiskey they called "schnapps," tossed back with a leer.

I have disliked buffets ever since.

It was a scene my grandfather Dave Pinsky would have scorned, and I knew for a fact that he had done battle with the institution. My father, his oldest son, studied briefly with the autocratic, legendary Rabbi Dardik, and soon became a discipline problem. The rabbi's ensuing conflict with Milford's father, the young gangster Dave Pinsky, ended in a shouting scene that made my father chuckle when he told me about it.

The strict contract of the Shema, at the heart of the rituals I remember, is a commitment to daily practice of the faith. To love God with all your heart and soul and strength, and to put reminders of that obligation on your hands and your eyes and your doorposts. Once you have experienced that obligation in a certain communal way, any formal or institutional compromise may seem impossible. Long after the reign of Dardik, the pulpit in my time belonged to Rabbi Kellman. In his sermons, he would reprimand Long Branch's infant but already prosperous Reform temple. Here in our shul, Rabbi Kellman said, on the Day of Atonement we blow the ram's horn shofar as commanded by God. Over there in the suburbs, he said, they keep the shofar in a glass case, with a label explaining that "our ancestors" blew it.

I had heard the Reform rabbi, Dr. Tartufkovich, speak at

an interfaith school assembly. In line with my family's prej-udices and Rabbi Kellman's scorn, I found the Reform rabbi slick and too well fed. He made being Jewish seem easy. If my bar mitzvah studies had taught me anything, it was that being Jewish was demanding, and if impossibly demanding—"all your heart and all your soul"—then alright, the impossible requirements were all the more a matter for pride.

Let the Protestants stand up and declare, "I have sinned"—of course you have. How could you not? We Jews assumed that no one can fulfill the totality of the Shema. The revamping of the Shema's severe expectations made Rabbi Tartufkov-ich and his happy compromises seem weak in a way that was not Jewish. Those Reform Jews were less Jewish even than Zaydee Pop, who, though he was a "bad Jew," was at least a bad Orthodox Jew. I could have imagined the same about Eartha Kitt or Charlie Chaplin.

My father had a story he liked about that disorderly syn-agogue scene. As a breadwinner who worked on Saturday mornings, he did not appear at the prolonged Sabbath ser-vices that a twelve-year-old like me was doomed to attend as "our family's representative." Like many in his generation, he annually attended the shul on the High Holy Days. One Yom Kippur, while the old men were voicing their competi-tive cantorial powers, bobbing and dipping their bodies, an out-of-town visitor next to my father turned to him and said, "I've never seen a shul like this!"

"Yes," said my father. "It's a real madhouse, isn't it?"

The stranger, looking at those oak pews and the stained-glass windows, was surprised.

"No, I mean it's so *beautiful*."

When my father was in his eighties, I wanted to ask him about these matters of idolatry and (to cite the Boy Scout's Oath) reverence. When Dave Pinsky died, I was barely twelve years old. My father was about thirty-five, a hardworking small businessman trying to make a go of his partnership with Kirk Pettiford. I had a memory I could not make sense of.

Faithfully, for the prescribed eleven months, my father—young, pragmatic, scraping to support his family, his wife not an eager helpmate—got out of bed before six every morning so he could walk to that Orthodox shul on Second Avenue. There, he recited the morning prayers and wrapped the leather tefillin around his arms and head and recited the Kaddish for the dead, in memory of his irreligious father. He did that every weekday for the prescribed eleven months, and after the service he walked directly to the offices of Milford S. Pinsky and P. Kirk Pettiford at the corner of Broadway and Third Avenue, to begin his demanding day at work.

Why? My father was a diligent person. He was treasurer of Long Branch's Salvation Army, as a practical, civic-minded citizen of his town's Broadway. I remember the kindly colonel who stored the Army's tripod and kettle in the back room of the optical office, where every weekday and Saturday Milford Pinsky worked from early in the morning till six at night, and till nine on Thursday nights. I can't recall a single word about religion from him, ever.

Why, then, did he perform that tedious, prolonged observance, those months of getting up early the morning in bondage to a daily ritual I knew for sure was not inspiring or sustaining for him? Did Zaydee Pop, with his family Christmas dinners and his big ornamented tree, have an unsuspected connection to Judaism? Did Dave Pinsky ever go to the shul to pray on Friday night or Saturday morning?

"No," said my father, when I asked him. "You know, he was a tough guy."

"Was he ever bar-mitzvahed?"

My father had no idea.

Then why in the world say kaddish for him for eleven months, winter and summer?

"Well . . . because he made me do it with him when my mother died."

Milford Simon Pinsky was a child of seven or eight at the time. Dave's bootlegging activities would have been near their height. There is a sentimental appeal in the picture of the youthful rum-runner, in his sporty clothes, taking his small son with him each weekday morning for nearly a year to say memorial prayers for his beautiful young wife, the boy's mother, Rose. As a love story, it might have added to the pain felt by Rose's replacement, her cousin Molly. Decades later, my father's observance seems to express respect toward both parents, perhaps toward the love story, and certainly toward the feelings of that bereaved child, his young self.

But in the strict terms of my haftorah, Isaiah 66, is that kind of respect in the spirit of acceptable worship? Or is it, rather, idolatry?

I think it is idolatry, because it is autonomously defined. "They have chosen their own ways," I sang unknowingly, "and their soul delighteth in their abominations." It is hard to deny that Dave in 1924 and Milford in 1951 chose their own ways of mourning their dead—impossible for me not to feel loyalty toward those autonomous choices.

On the other hand, the Lord whose throne is heaven and footstool the earth finds the flaw in even elaborate worship, the incense that is like blessing an idol, the sacrifice that is like cutting a dog's neck. Only the humble spirit that trembles at God's word is not idolatrous. "Humble spirit" does not describe Dave Pinsky as people saw him. Whether it justly describes the spirit in which he recited the kaddish for his first wife, God knows. We can think that when flesh mourns for flesh—parent or lover—it must be humble, having tasted its own end, in its mourning.

In the terrible final words of the Book of Isaiah, the chosen few who are virtuous in the eyes of the Lord witness the doom of the transgressors:

> *And they shall go forth, and look upon the carcasses of the men*
> *that have transgressed against me: for their worm shall not*
> *die, neither shall their fire be quenched; and they shall be an*
> *abhorring unto all flesh.*

It is horrible and comical to imagine a child on the thresh-old of puberty singing these words to a congregation, sup-posedly sealing his admission into a community of worship he more than half knows he will soon leave. The beauty of chanting words with their meaning mostly inaccessible, with every flame-shaped character on the scroll related to breath—somewhere in that maimed ceremony was an avenue toward poetry. As James Baldwin says:

"One cannot claim the birthright without accepting the inheritance."

XI

Teacher

O
N MARCH 15, 1945, Paul Fussell, a lieutenant in the
103rd Infantry Division, who would later become my
teacher at Rutgers, underwent an intense barrage of
German artillery, lying facedown in a clearing alongside his
platoon sergeant and military tutor, Edward Keith Hudson.
Fussell was twenty years old. Hudson was thirty-seven.

Fussell wrote vividly about that day in a 1982 piece for
Harper's entitled "My War":

> I was psychologically and morally ill prepared to lead my
> platoon in the great Seventh Army attack of March 15,
> 1945. But lead it I did, or rather push it, staying as far in
> the rear as was barely decent. And before the day was over
> I had been severely rebuked by a sharp-eyed lieutenant-
> colonel who threatened court martial if I didn't pull myself
> together. Before that day was over I was sprayed with the
> contents of a soldier's torso when I was lying behind him
> and he knelt to fire at a machine gun holding us up: he
> was struck in the heart, and out of the holes in the back of
> his field jacket flew little clouds of tissue, blood, and pow-

dered cloth. Near him another man raised himself to fire, but the machine gun caught him in the mouth, and as he fell he looked back at me with surprise, blood and teeth dribbling out onto the leaves. He was one to whom early on I had given the Silver Star for heroism, and he didn't want to let me down.

A German shell wounded Fussell terribly all down the back of his body. The same shell killed Sergeant Hudson, the working-class older man who had forgiven young Lieutenant Fussell many mistakes, while teaching him how to lead a rifle platoon.

Facedown, pressed against one another, the two men were holding hands. That was a custom for mutual reassurance, as Fussell in his old age explained to an interviewer: reassurance that neither of the two men would run away—as many officers had done. So my teacher says for the camera, his old man's voice rising on the plural noun in rage and contempt. Edward Keith Hudson's violent death, he says in the same interview "is behind everything I've done."

I tend to avoid the word "mentor." For many people, it is a good, honorable term, the name of a wise instructor in the *Odyssey*. But the word sometimes has a corporate or cultish feeling. Loftier and more important, in my personal vocabulary, is "teacher." Katherine Lane, Elizabeth Gibbs, Angus McWithey, Ada Judson, Frances Ferguson, Laurence Ryan, Yvor Winters and Paul Fussell have been my teachers. They didn't foster my career or show me professional ropes. They taught me things.

I've learned from friends older than me, too, but I'd rather call Thom Gunn a friend than a mentor. When we were Berkeley colleagues, Thom showed me how to see the great and small failings in yourself and other people without sentimentality, so the clarity might lead you toward acceptance, or even love, not judgment. Once I told him, in an apologetic way, that I regretted reading one of my poems for the second or third time when he was in the audience.

"You know, Robert," said Thom, "I know what you mean—but it's a bit silly. I don't have your poems by heart. Probably no one at your poetry reading does. If a poem is any good at all, it's useful to hear it more than once."

Paul Fussell the wealthy Californian who lived in Princeton, and Thom Gunn the English gay man who lived in San Francisco, were different from one another—and from me. But in my twenties and in my forties, at Rutgers and at Berkeley, they both showed me what poetry has to do with the rest of life.

In 1959, when Fussell became my second-semester teacher in what was called an Honors Section of Freshman Composition, I didn't know anything about his war experiences. He had not yet written his celebrated book *The Great War and Modern Memory*, dedicated "To the Memory of Technical Sergeant Edward Keith Hudson, ASN 36558772 Co., F, 410th Infantry / Killed beside me in France / March 15, 1945."

What we students saw in our composition class was a tall, fair-haired, elegantly dressed man in his thirties. Gray blazer, expensive shoes, Parliament cigarettes with recessed filters. He had selected us for this elite, small group. Counterbalancing any pride we might take in that status, he addressed us with an opaque, not-quite-scornful irony. Fussell respected our intelligence, that tone implied, and he was amused by our ignorance.

In the years to come, many books emerged from that bunch of state university freshmen. Peter Najarian's published fiction includes *Voyages*, a memorable novel of Armenian immigrant life. Henry Dumas's poetry is a landmark for young Black poets I know. Henry died ten years after our Honors class—shot dead in the New York subway by a transit cop who said he was defending himself against Henry, although it turns out (so the cop testified) he mistook Henry for somebody else.

As I type that sentence I struggle, among many other emotions, to think lucidly about the brief haven—or was it a vivarium, or a stage set?—that made us all a group of friends, proud of our selection by Fussell in that postwar state university classroom. An island in our culture, and in the nightmare of history.

Now, in my eighties, I have heard friends and colleagues, Black and white, criticize the concept of white privilege in various reasonable ways. For example, have the words become a slogan that substitutes for action? The phrase has a kind of absolute validity for me, going back to childhood, when white privilege was an obvious, bewildering reality visible every day at the corner of Rockwell Avenue and Monmouth.

I can't be sure how much that feeling is reinforced by the fact that in 1968 Henry was killed by a police officer who claimed both self-defense and mistaken identity, whereas I have had a long and, as the saying goes, charmed life. "Privilege" may be too mild an understatement as I think back to Henry's death, his talent, his writing and his place in our composition class.

My best friend in the group, Robert Maniquis, a chain-smoking and elegantly chain-talking Filipino show-off, became a professor at UCLA, a world-class expert on the literature of the French Revolution. Even back then Maniquis could speak French and German with apparent ease, and he confidently used phrases like "a priori" and "diametrically opposed." He had graduated from New Brunswick High School, and knew the college town well, having grown up near the Rutgers campus.

Most of us, as first-year students at a land-grant state university, were required to spend two years in (but not of) ROTC—

the Reserve Officers Training Corps. The only exceptions in our Honors Composition class were Henry Dumas, who had already been in the Air Force, and Kenny Garelick, who at fifteen was too young for ROTC.

Every semester, for all two years of that compulsory ROTC class we were required to attend in uniform, both Bob Maniquis and I received the minimum passing grade of D. I remember Bob suddenly shouting from his desk, in the middle of a lecture about a new military policy called, with initial caps, "the New Pentomic Army"—the official phrase for using small-scale, tactical nuclear weapons in battle. Our startled teacher, Captain Hess, asked him to explain himself. Still wearing the dark lenses that hid his eyes while he slept in class, Maniquis explained that he had awoken from a bad dream.

Every spring a fraternity house named something like Delta Phi or Chi Psi displayed from its second-floor balcony an immense Confederate flag. And every spring Maniquis and I, over coffees at the New Brunswick Lunch, devoted prolonged sessions to plotting ways we would steal or incinerate that flag. Nighttime ladders, lighter fluid and flaming arrows were discussed, along with ploys like posing as plumbing inspectors. To our shame and regret, we never did it.

Possibly because we were pretentious in similar ways, and were together so much, people often slipped and addressed him as "Pinsky" or called me "Maniquis," though we looked nothing alike. In standard behavior for our type of freshman, he and I took pride in going to the movies on the night before English papers were due. After the movie, our custom was a discussion over leisurely omelets and more coffee back at the New Brunswick Lunch before returning to our portable typewriters for more conversation, more coffee, no sleep, and delivery of our work, just on time, to class the next morning.

That juvenile showing-off had an extra edge of elitism

because the Rutgers of those days dealt with being a state university by admitting a large freshman class—more than half were dropped out before the end of the first year. Our capers and last-minute A's were a way for Maniquis and me to affirm that we were special.

Among other subjects during those late-night omelets we discussed Princeton University, sixteen miles away. The students there, we decided, were male WASPs who had successfully completed the obedience training of their social class—a group we disdained as our inferiors. They were further beneath us, in our own eyes, than the Rutgers ROTC boys who polished their shoes and brass buttons in doomed hope that an A in ROTC might let them avoid flunking out of Rutgers. Maniquis and I chose to look on ourselves as underdog nobility—like Ivanhoe, you might say, though we didn't go that far.

This undefined superiority was bolstered by a popular book published while we were in high school, based on the personal attitudes (obnoxious, complacent) of anonymous Princeton undergraduates. I had read excerpts in one of those magazines in the optical waiting room. It didn't occur to my friend and me that in our way we were as self-centered as those preening, nameless jerks from down the road.

The great Paul Robeson, Maniquis and I liked knowing, grew up in the town of Princeton, but graduated from Rutgers—not Princeton, where (except for the seminary) hardly any person of Robeson's race had ever graduated. The much later days of Michelle Obama as a Princeton student, or of a Jewish man named Shapiro becoming the university's president, were far in the unimagined future. Paul Fussell shrewdly played into our prejudices by observing that Princeton (where he lived), with its downtown of pseudo-Georgian storefronts, actually contained fewer eighteenth century buildings than we had in funky, urban New Brunswick.

As I remember, we never tried our all-night paper-writing routine with Fussell. Each week he announced who was the new "champion": the author of the previous week's best paper. Questionable teaching in many ways, but for earnest poseurs like Bob Maniquis and me (he had ceded me possession of "Robert") our teacher's weekly announcement of first prize probably made us try harder. The childish competition emphasized the supreme or crucial importance of writing. Like many in our generation, we joined a worshipful cult around Joyce's *A Portrait of the Artist as a Young Man*. The sexist, patriarchal appeal of the last word in that title seems, in retrospect, a high-art version of a general devotion to Ernest Hemingway.

If I had read our teacher's account of slaughtered and wounded Americans and Germans of about our age, I might not have described the ethnic variety of our group the way I sometimes did, glibly comparing it to a rifle platoon in a war movie. Fussell never in my hearing referred to his war experience. Rank was present, indirectly, in the fact that he called us Mr. Pinsky, Mr. Maniquis, Mr. Najarian and Mr. Dumas, just as we called him Mr. Fussell. I liked that a lot. The formality, in contrast with the infantilizing "Robert" from Mr. McWithey, Miss Judson and Mr. Pulaski in high school, seemed both egalitarian and classy. To be "Mr." seemed to recognize and challenge my veneer of self-confidence, and the underlying gulfs of despair. It felt like the opposite of being graded for "Citizenship" on high school report cards.

The show-off rebellion that got me bad grades in high school subsided at Rutgers, aside from a few throwback incidents. First semester of freshman year, the teacher in my history class asked me to leave the room when I persisted in contradicting him about something. I can't remember what the issue was, and he probably did the right thing, no matter how much my bad manners resembled the kind of writing I went on to do. That same semester, I was enraged by a final examination in political science that asked only that the students regurgitate exactly what had been said in class. No window for improvisation or understanding; the test would give A+ to a tape recorder. I showed my disdain by completing the two-hour exam in twenty minutes. I turned in my blue-book answers with a sneer, and got a grade of B-.

Fussell recognized expertise in different people. Mr. Najarian, whose cousin Arthur Pinajian was a painter, had haunted the Museum of Modern Art and knew a lot about modern and contemporary painters. Mr. Dumas had grown up a minister's son and with wry detachment he could explain biblical references. He also knew a bit about Arabic cultures. He confided in me that he felt in many ways like a phony—his father-in-law, in particular, saw right through him, he said. Mr. Maniquis, in contrast, enjoyed being an open, brilliant bullshitter. He had read a remarkable amount of philosophy and knew how to seem as if he had read even more. Mr. Garelick, our fifteen-year-old prodigy, had a smart pre-med major's knowledge of science. I knew (or could pretend to know) a little about jazz.

But my real moment came when we got to poetry. Not that I knew much, but when Fussell asked Mr. Pinsky to please read aloud Marianne Moore's poem "Silence," a recognition happened. Paul Fussell had written his Harvard doctoral thesis on eighteenth century prosody. He could hear that although I was ignorant of the terminology, I understood the relation of pitch to quantity, of sentence-melody to line and, in a non-actor way, the relation of all that harmony, melody and rhythm to meaning. Fussell recognized that in me, and by letting me know that he did, he helped me recognize it in myself.

That ability of ear is like something in music or sports—not that you are great, but that you can sing harmony, or you can run fast or jump high. I have recognized it in young poets—sometimes much younger than I was in Fussell's class. I have recognized it even in graduate students who natter about literary theory or about the typography of their poems on a printed page. Some of them can also hear.

And hearing makes meaning possible. It's a little like what Dizzy Gillespie says in his *Paris Review* interview, about the ability "to see [his mischievous verb!] two or three rhythms going at once." It's "how you accent," he says, "where your accents are and how they fit in with different types of rhythm." That unmistakable knack called "ear" is only a beginning. Accent—formal emphasis, sometimes two or three strains of it at once—builds emotion. On great subjects, such as King Lear welcoming the harshness of nature, Emily Dickinson feeling the personal contortions of time, William Butler Yeats asserting the spiritual coherence of art, meaning becomes a physical presence.

With his excellent clothes and his fastidious, satirical tone, Paul Fussell could be absurd, in an admirable mode of self-parody. He read aloud to us Matthew Arnold's paragraph about the remarkable ugliness of certain hideous English surnames: "Higginbottom, Stiggins, Bugg," our teacher drawled, of course adding, after an amused pause, "Fussell." Decades later, I thought of that moment when the novelist Alan Cheuse, another Fussell student, told me that when Alan mentioned my name, Fussell responded with, "Ah yes. Pinsky—one of my very best creations."

An interesting remark. Why did Fussell, who already had academic tenure, decide to teach freshman composition? Possibly instead of a graduate course? Even the time and effort he spent going through our first-semester work, consulting our teachers to make his selections for the Honors Section—as he clearly had done personally—meant extra effort for him. If I had thought about his motivation at the time, I might have said, fatuously, that he wanted to teach the cream of the crop, a small and select group.

Maybe so, or maybe he was just avoiding some less attractive teaching assignment. But I think his motivation went deeper. Interviewed in the Ken Burns video series about war, Fussell says he was grateful for Basic Training because it gave him his first encounter with people who worked for a living. He describes how those working-class soldiers were kind to an unimpressive, overweight rich boy.

We various Rutgers boys Fussell selected for his special composition class were about the same age as those soldiers, and we came from families that worked for a living. We also were the same age as the war dead he remembered. In his book *Doing Battle*, Fussell describes getting lost one night with the rifle platoon he commanded, so lost that they went to sleep on the ground where they were in the pitch-dark, moonless woods. Waking up the next morning, he discovers that he and his men have been sleeping among objects he recognizes, after a moment, as "dozens of dead German boys in greenish gray uniforms, killed a day or two before by the company we were replacing." "Boys": He could not forget the youth of the German corpses that were next to him and his soldiers all night.

I prefer mixing to purity in many things. I don't see much good in single-sex education, especially all-male college education, which was still the regime when I was a student at Rutgers, the State University of New Jersey. But inside the university's defective, outmoded single-sex system, Dumas and Najarian and Maniquis and I reaped rewards that could be traced back to the Battle of the Bulge. Paul Fussell believed deeply, with an angry conviction, in public education at the highest level. I can remember him, in a walk across campus, scolding a student who had tossed an empty cigarette pack onto the pathway. Calmly, the eminent skeptic and satirist told the kid to respect where he was.

I don't mean to idealize Fussell. He was a lifelong snob. He claimed that when anyone said to him, "Have a nice day," he always responded, "Thank you, but I have other plans." The war deepened and refined his snobbery by extending it to contempt for noncombatant delusions that falsified the immoral, obscene nature of war. Skillfully, he used his superiority about vague, trite, incorrect, inflated or stupid language to teach us about writing. The snobbery and the shameless fomenting of competition among his students could get obnoxious, but I am grateful for how well Fussell made his personality into a technique for driving us toward learning. Intellectual rigor and clarity, with enough work, might improve even our understanding of ourselves.

What we his students witnessed was Fussell's creation of his own character, a being forged by American social prejudice and elevated by the transforming ugliness of war. We benefited from that performance without understanding it. I'll quote a passage from his 1982 *Harper's* piece that would have astounded us innocent freshmen:

> How did an upper-middle-class young gentleman find himself in so unseemly a place? Why wasn't he in the Navy, at least, or in the OSS or Air Corps administration or editing *Stars and Stripes* or being a general's aide? The answer is comic: at the age of twenty I found myself leading forty riflemen over the Vosges Mountains and watching them being torn apart by German artillery and machine guns because when I was sixteen, in junior college, I was fat and flabby, with feminine tits and a big behind. For years the thing I'd hated most about school was gym, for there I was obliged to strip and shower communally. Thus I chose to join the ROTC (infantry, as it happened) because that was a way to get out of gym, which meant you never had to take off your clothes and invite—indeed, compel—ridicule.

In the Ken Burns interview he explains that in the course of Basic Training, with the help of the new friends he made there, he lost twenty pounds. Because his name on military documents was "Paul Fussell, Jr." they nicknamed him "Junior," and accepted him. Those young men and Sergeant Hudson did not displace Fussell's early snobbery, but they let him make something good out of it. His fellow soldiers added to that defensively scornful personality something much better, beyond the affected superiority of the rich, fat child—no matter how much that child, too, was always there.

Strange to say, Fussell's view of the world in certain ways resembled those shared by my mother and father. Like those penniless children of immigrants in New Jersey, the well-off former fat boy from California was deeply skeptical of worldly honors and distinctions, medals and hierarchies. (He drew a funny, shrewd set of equivalents between military and academic ranks.) As Milford and Sylvia took seriously yet scorned the ability to buy a split-level house in Elberon, Paul took seriously yet scorned the regulations and hierarchies of the military and academic worlds. Like my parents, the infantryman Fussell didn't mistake the world's prizes and hierarchies for anything real. Like them, he had no illusions about official distinctions, and like them he understood the practical value of such things.

Like it or not, every institution—the Army, a profession, a school—assigns an identity. Before I met Fussell, Maniquis, Dumas and the others, when I was still in high school, in the years before Rutgers and an hour's drive away, my identity was: saxophone player.

XII

Music

MELODRAMATIC THOUGH it sounds to say so, the horn in a sense did save my life. For a few years in my adolescence, I was incapable of doing things I was supposed to do. I could read anything in the history textbook, except for the assigned passages, the task at hand. That inability was already deep in me by kindergarten. Thanks to my mother, who saved the report card, I can quote my first-grade teacher at the Garfield School, Miss Phillips, in her exact words. "Robert is always courteous" she says, but also:

> . . . he has taken to dreaming and talking to himself. He doesn't keep his mind on the job at hand . . . He seems to draw within himself much of the time.

The "talking to himself" included talking to (or as) imaginary beings and inanimate objects, to books and to absent people. Talking, including the language of politeness, was the best way to parry fear or sadness. Writing begins, says Sigmund Freud, as the voice of an absent person. My own voice gave me a protective social absence, in the cloak of artful speech.

By the seventh grade, as the first wisps of hair sprouted on my upper lip, at school I started to talk too much, and out of turn. "Thinking aloud" would be a mild way to describe it. Instead of quietly doing nothing, or cheating on tests like a sensible person, I began to make polite, aggressive little speeches about what was wrong, or pointless, in our assigned work. Or I volunteered corrections. One of the few examples I can recall was when a teacher thought the biblical name Shadrach might be related to shad roe. "Mr. Kolibas," I said, "excuse me, but I'm surprised at your ignorance."

In a town like Long Branch, the career choice to become a teacher was often made by someone born to immigrant parents in a wage-dependent family. To become a doctor or a lawyer took more money and more years than to become a teacher. People only a generation removed from the bottom of a social ladder can be cautious about calling attention to themselves at work or in school. They have reasons to place a high value on doing your job without complaining, while cooperating with authority. Don't talk back or show off.

First-generation professionals in the United States will not necessarily approve of a thirteen-year-old wiseacre who talks a lot and acts smart. For the eighth-grade year at Long Branch Junior High School, I was placed in a remedial or punitive classroom with some official name. Everybody knew it as the Dumb Class, or the Bad Class: a source of despair concealed under a mask of cocky indifference.

But I had started playing the horn, the one thing I was recognized for being any good at. I enjoyed sports, but I was no better than average. I did not get good grades. But at school dances and eventually at parties and weddings and bar mitzvahs and then at bars, I could play music that people danced to and could hear without groaning. My breath supplied the melody, while a roomful of people enjoyed themselves. I liked that.

I got that ability just in time. For generations the main music teacher in Long Branch schools was Mr. Winthrop, a gruff, impatient man with a pronounced European accent. Years later I realized that he was an immigrant, probably a refugee once named Weintraub. The *Mayflower*-sounding name suited his local celebrity. In Long Branch, the mailman and the dentist and the bartender might well have learned an instrument as students of Mr. Winthrop when they were kids. They respected his brusque authority, and so did I.

Mr. Winthrop had an efficient but unsanitary way to decide who would get those free music lessons, with free use of a beginner instrument. At his desk facing a roomful of children, he put onto the desk the mouthpiece for a trumpet or for a clarinet, depending on whether he was filling slots in woodwind or brass that day. He asked each of us to pick up the mouthpiece, executing either the buzzy pucker for brass or, for woodwind, the tongue-directed plosion of air at the taut cushion of lower lip over bottom teeth. If you produced an audible squawk or honk you were accepted. When it was my turn I picked up that germ-filled clarinet mouthpiece and made a noise.

The successor to old Mr. Winthrop was young Mr. Soriano. Years later, in Florida for the Festival of the Arts Boca, I met an excellent trumpet player who was from Long Branch. That professional musician and I agreed that our town had been blessed with Dom Soriano, who had a long career as an inspiring teacher in the public schools.

Soon after he arrived in town, Mr. Soriano noticed my playing for kids dancing in the gym at lunchtime. It was me on horn, with a drummer and a stand-up bass player, doing versions of Chuck Berry and Elvis Presley hits and things like "Night Train" or Clifford Scott's tenor solo on Bill Doggett's "Honky Tonk, Parts I & II." Dom Soriano responded by giving me solos in some band performances. At one concert, he had me stand in front of the band at a mic, wearing sunglasses

and holding my horn while I delivered a silly hipster monologue somebody (not me!) had written.

Playing music was my main refuge from myself, from the
despairing and arrogant character who talked to himself and
ignored the task at hand and wound up in the Dumb Class.
I didn't know how to get good grades. Maybe the horn was
a refuge from my family, too, or from life with other people
in general. I kept getting a grade of D in Citizenship, which
offended my patriotism. I made speeches about how it should
be called Deportment.

Music helped. My grades got a little better, or less bad,
each year. It was an unhappy phase, but in a way I am still
thankful for those Cs and Ds that schooled me in looking
beyond institutional awards. Other pleasures go deeper:
making music with other people, the joy of listening to one
another and to yourself within the ensemble. Making music
can be the opposite of loneliness.

For many years, I thought that pleasure was behind me,
until the producer and editor Richard Connolly got me into
a studio with the pianist Laurence Hobgood. A new phase
began for me with the PoemJazz recordings, and in performances with Laurence and others. That first day, Laurence
had studied the poems and began saying insightful things
about them. Harking back to what I learned from Mr. Soriano, I suggested that we just begin, trusting the sounds to
guide us. Laurence put the texts of the poems on the easel of
the piano, I went to my microphone in a booth where I could
see him, and we began. Some of the tracks from that day are
on the first PoemJazz CD, and an old, particular joy came
back as though from the dead.

Another pleasure in those sometimes miserable teenager
days was learning Spanish, which was taught by the football
coach Army Ippolito, a classmate of my mother's and father's
when they were all at Long Branch High. In Army's class, I

did pretty well in conversation—like music, it cheered me up—but not so well on the quizzes. Joyce Henderson and I were among the few kids in Army's class who didn't have the declensions and conjugations and irregular verbs written on their inner forearms, or in microscopic ballpoint on a pink eraser. Joyce was too moral to cheat that way, and I was too disorganized and scornful to cheat more than once in a while. Joyce always got an A in Spanish, and I always got something between a B- and a D+.

Army Ippolito seemed puzzled by that. He and my mother had graduated high school the same year. She reported that when she ran into him downtown, Army told her that I bewildered him by shining in conversation but not on the quizzes.

"Your son," he said to her, "doesn't want to get an A."

"So you know what I told him?" she said. "I told him, 'That's okay, Army. Sooner or later, the cream always rises to the top.'"

It's reasonable to find Sylvia Pinsky's response to Army Ippolito repellent. My secret grief was, I knew Army was right about me. Defying the sources of recognition, I needed to defeat myself and I couldn't understand why. Sylvia did have a good point about there being values higher than A. But why make failure into a badge? Would it kill me to learn the conjugations?

Another athletic coach, a young gym teacher named Pulaski, took a terrific dislike to me. In my senior year he was faculty adviser to the sophomore class. As leader of a little band, I attended a meeting where the sophomore class was planning their spring dance. I don't remember how much the sophomores were going to pay us musicians, but as their class adviser, Mr. Pulaski overruled the students. It was too much money. So I said that I personally would take no money. They only had to pay the pianist and the drummer. Again, the faculty adviser overruled the students. Still too much money.

"Okay," I said. "We will all play for free as our donation to the sophomore class of Long Branch Senior High School." There was nothing Mr. Pulaski could do. He was furious.

I have never matured completely beyond conflicts like that one between a hardworking, somewhat authoritarian coach and teacher on one side and an inwardly desperate, outwardly arrogant teenage saxophone player on the other. I still get into similar kerfuffles. A certain kind of A, sometimes, is not for me. Mr. Pulaski keeps appearing in new forms, and I keep taking the bait. Maybe, as they say about comedians, practicing a vocal art is rooted in aggression and need, reaching far back past adolescence into the plaintive, distressed, infantile origins of a human voice.

With my band's gig settled, no matter what Mr. Pulaski wanted, I politely excused myself and left that meeting of the sophomore class. Another young teacher followed me into the hall. I wish I could remember her name. She had something to tell me.

"*Don't let him bully you!*" she said.

That same teacher, the following year, became Mrs. Pulaski. She must have known exactly what she was talking about.

I had been playing in an after-school volleyball game that included faculty and students. The football player Stan Wheeler, who had brought me into the game, told me Mr. Pulaski asked him not to bring me anymore.

"It's not because of his religion," Pulaski told Stan, and I actually think that was true, pretty much.

The next fall, my college board scores got me into Rutgers, despite my poor grades overall and in Citizenship. Thanks to Dom Soriano, I passed my audition for the college's jazz and marching bands. It didn't take much practice to play "76 Trombones" while marching in the weekly ROTC drills. The same went for playing the repetitious, simplified big band charts for jazz band. I began practicing the horn less.

A few times, little music jobs came up. At a party, fraternity boys and their dates danced while another middling horn player and I performed with a drummer and a really excellent piano player. We played a hundred choruses of the Symphony Sid theme, in the tenor player's congenial key of F-natural. We horn players that night weren't very good, either of us, but we played loud and we kept time. I hope the good piano player admired our nerve.

I was going through a conversion, giving more time to poetry than to the saxophone. "Sailing to Byzantium" by William Butler Yeats got into me. I typed out the poem and taped it onto the wall above my toaster. Without noticing, I got it by heart.

Yeats's "artifice of eternity" stunned me with its final assurance to include everything: "what is past, or passing, or to come," not just the world of art, but the entire, actual world where art is the supreme element. Language-drunk, I made a concoction of Byzantium and Stephen Dedalus's formula. The artifice of eternity might be a way to awake from the nightmare of history. Yeats's poem embodied a spiritual power—a secular spiritual power—with powers beyond two entities that once threatened to form me: Christianity and Judaism, mighty episodes of the nightmare from which I would try to awake.

Those religions were trying to tell me who I was. In resisting their forces, I felt that "Sailing to Byzantium" was on my side, a conviction that formed before I learned anything about Yeats's crazy, homemade religion of art. The poem had a possessed confidence I loved in, say, Illinois Jacquet playing Thelonious Monk's " 'Round Midnight" on the bassoon. The goofy, improvised mysticism of the Irish poet was transformed by the authority of music, in the form of verse.

(Ottava rima, to be specific, though I didn't know the term.) In the poem that entered my memory unwilled I heard its happy authority, a grace beyond anything I found in the two great religions.

A brilliant graduate student named Fred Tremallo befriended Henry Dumas, Peter Najarian and me. I think Tremallo and Dumas were neighbors. Ten years older than me, well read and smart, Fred was the first grown-up, ambitious writer I knew. When he saw my typed-out copy of "Sailing to Byzantium" posted on the kitchen wall, Fred Tremallo said the poem was good, but there was no point in the rhyme, that old-fashioned delusion that still afflicted Yeats and his generation. That conversation was an example of his kindness to us brats, but I knew he was missing something vital about Yeats's poem and about poetry itself. Tremallo was wrong.

A couple of times I made the one-hour drive back to the Shore from Rutgers, to play little jobs with the musicians I had worked with in high school. One occasion finished that for good. My friends had set up an audition to play weekend nights in the cocktail lounge of a German restaurant in Atlantic Highlands. The manager wanted something more sophisticated than the oompah band that played polkas for customers eating sauerbraten and schnitzel in their main dining room.

I decided the job called for playing ballads on the clarinet, which I had been practicing even less than the saxophone. I stank up the place. My high school musician friends and I got through that Friday evening but they did not get the job.

On the drive back home to Rutgers after that humiliating audition, I realized that my grandiose fantasies were no longer about being a musician. Seemingly overnight, they had become grandiose fantasies of being a poet. Reciting "Sailing to Byzantium" to myself, I decided to do as the poem says.

Once out of nature, I would never take my bodily form from any natural thing. What do those words mean? Without being able to say precisely, I relate "bodily form" to Ralph Ellison's distinction between relatives and ancestors. You choose your ancestors, he says in his essay on Richard Wright. Wright was a "relative," says Ellison, and Ernest Hemingway was an "ancestor." The Irish writers Joyce and Yeats were not my relatives in nature, but in the workings of form—form, that mysterious refuge from despair—could I choose them as my ancestors?

In a much-anthologized poem by Yeats, "John Kinsella's Lament for Mrs. Mary Moore," I had noted the words "Though stiff to strike a bargain, / Like an old Jew Man." I felt no surprise at that small, essentially familiar example of bigotry or stereotyping in history's imaginative nightmare. In a spirit of neither revenge nor submission, why not try to adopt Yeats as an ancestor, along with the anti-semitic T. S. Eliot and Ezra Pound, as well as honoring James Joyce for making his Ulysses a secular Jew?

Some people might indict my relation to those ancestral writers (and many more, including Ellison himself) as an act of self-colonization: bending my neck to the yoke of a majority Christian culture. Or was it an act of cultural appropriation? I might prefer to call it breaking-and-entering. I respect my students who say they value having models in art and life who, as the saying goes, "look like me." Yes. I have felt something comparable. The opposite has also been true. White though we all were, the Irish writers—the scholarly, driven expatriate Catholic and the twilight-ridden Anglo-Irish Protestant snob—did not, in a cultural way, "look" like me.

In quotation marks or not, even the plain, one-syllable verb "look" has its nightmare history. Do people look Jewish, or not? Does the idea of looking Jewish recall old-time comedy in movies and vaudeville?—or similar images in lethal

Nazi caricatures, still circulating, maybe more than ever, in the United States?

Depending on how you look at it, the figurative ancestors Joyce and Yeats might or might not resemble my actual ancestors and me. But nevertheless I was learning the ways that they were me, and that I was them. For Dumas, Maniquis and me and the others in our Honors Composition platoon, part of Fussell's effectiveness as a teacher was similar. He did not look like us, in different ways, and he was one of us. He and I were Marianne Moore, when I recited those lines by her, as a tributary current in my conversion from practicing one art to another.

Saying that my transition from saxophone to poetry happened overnight may seem dismissive, a confession of my youthful triviality. But what I try to do in my poems is almost exactly what I wanted to do with the horn. I loved the sound of returning to a theme with more emotion each time with each chorus, building, turning or expanding. The jazz players I looked up to might begin with some ordinary tune or sequence of chords they transported, by extremes of sweat and surprise, into a specific heaven. Same with Yeats or Ginsberg or Dickinson. To emulate that feeling, feebly or not, was a thrill. If the few dollars I earned playing my horn at a fraternity party paid for one or two poetry books I bought at Shelley's College Book Store, that was a fitting swerve.

I turned my clumsy but heartfelt attention from music to poetry—embracing a lifetime of work I didn't know I had been hiding from, yet pursuing, for a long time.

XIII

Moving Around

*L*IFE STUDIES is Robert Lowell's best-known and most influential book. It won the National Book Award for poetry in 1960. I read it in 1962 and I hated it. In a shallow way, my dislike was a matter of social class. I said aloud to Lowell's book, "Yeah, I had a grandfather, too." Like my fellow would-be urban Beatniks at Rutgers, I preferred the manners of Allen Ginsberg's "Kaddish"—the poet reading the Hebrew prayer for the dead while listening to Ray Charles and walking the streets of Greenwich Village.

A year later, when I arrived as a graduate student at Stanford, I entered a culture more bucolic than what I had known at Rutgers, the State University of New Jersey—the home state of Ginsberg, with urban New Brunswick about an hour from those Village streets. Surrounding the sleepy Palo Alto of those days, an actual village, the future Silicon Valley was still a place of horse ranches and apricot orchards. Leland and Jane Stanford had founded the university on their ranch, in 1891, and the school's affectionate nickname for itself was "the Farm." In Palo Alto, too, as in the quite different literary and urban terrain of Rutgers, Robert Lowell's poetry was not held in the first rank of importance.

But five or six years later, in 1970, I took a job teaching at Wellesley College, not far from Boston and Cambridge, where I met poets who considered *Life Studies* a major work of art. For my impressive new friends Frank Bidart, Gail Mazur and Lloyd Schwartz, Lowell was the great living model of a poet. *Life Studies* had been transforming for them. A book I didn't like, and for years ignored, had opened new possibilities for people I admired.

Rejecting *Life Studies* on first encounter was partly a conventional reflex, an automatic dislike for inherited privilege. But the resistance I felt goes deeper, involving qualities of idiom and imagery, and—even more—their cultural implications. In the personal narratives and declarations of *Life Studies*, many readers valued a directness that for me lacked an antic, disjunctive quality I prized in American life and poetry. Lowell's autobiographical poems felt humorless and foursquare. They were not enough like the movies of Mel Brooks or the eruptive comic strips of Walt Kelly.

It was not just social class. Leaving aside laugh-out-loud comedy, an example in poetry of what I mean is the work of Marianne Moore. The social voice in her poem "Silence" is not exactly working class or ethnic. On the contrary, that poem begins:

> My father used to say,
> "Superior people never make long visits,
> have to be shown Longfellow's grave
> or the glass flowers at Harvard . . ."

After quoting her father's distinctly upper-middle-class assertion, Moore presents a memorably outlandish, inexplicable image for self-reliance: a cat with "the mouse's limp tail hanging like a shoelace from its mouth." The image comes from left field, mixing different registers of attention (Longfellow, glass flowers, shoelace) with an insouciance I find inspiring. Lowell, I thought, would never come up with that cat.

The oblique collision Moore creates between her father's social place and the cat's prey has a quality I admire in the work of Alan Dugan, whose *Poems* and *Poems 2* came out around the same time as *Life Studies*. Dugan's books were much more my speed. His (possibly legendary) ancestor Old Billy Blue Balls was wounded so he had "two ass-holes." Dugan has him say, "The North won the Civil War / without much help from me / although I wear a proof / of the war's obscenity" ("Fabrication of Ancestors."). *Life Studies* was more decorous.

The manic moods of Dugan, Ginsberg and Moore in their different ways included a sense of the ridiculous. Lowell's mania felt more somber and grand. Maybe those other poets were simply more appealing for a child of Sylvia Pinsky, with her rude jokes about Ruthie Edelstein's ass filling up a picture window—not a Lowell image.

Another poet I valued more than Lowell was Elizabeth Bishop. Her poetry had a recklessly candid darkness I loved. For example, the lonely interior landscape Bishop creates in "Crusoe in England"—a symbolic self-portrait without vanity—is not heroic or wistful. The island is harsh, monotonous, infertile and volcanic. More directly autobiographical, the childhood memory of Bishop's "In the Waiting Room" has a humdrum surface so completely realized that it can contain "rivulets of fire," cannibalism ("long pig") and horrifying breasts. Bishop's tough, sardonic way of writing about herself was bracing.

In the same spirit, I relished Dugan's "How We Heard the Name," a poem in the voice of a drunken soldier floating downriver on a log, addressing locals gaping at him from the banks of the river. Floating by, along with that laughing soldier and his log, are:

> dead horses, dead men
> and military debris,
> indicative of war
> or official acts upstream

The pair "war / or official acts" pleased me, and I liked how the river was also history and how the laughing, disrespectful soldier was also Alan Dugan himself.

Over the years, I mostly outgrew my dissenting first impression of *Life Studies*. I learned to appreciate the somber, restless music, for example, of "Skunk Hour," with "A car radio bleats / "Love, O careless love," and the garbage-scavenging mother skunk in the book's last lines that "jabs her wedgehead in a cup / of sour cream, drops her ostrich tail, / and will not scare."

Was my difference from those Cambridge friends partly regional? After I left Wellesley, returning to California in 1980, I discovered my Berkeley students were indifferent to Lowell's work. Theirs was a mellow version of my irritation with all those proper names, lines like "The farm, entitled *Char-de-sa* / in the Social Register, / was named for my Grandfather's children," in a poem entitled "My Last Afternoon with Uncle Devereux Winslow." The young Californians in my Berkeley classes didn't say to the book, "Yeah, I had an uncle too." Mildly, they explained to one another that Lowell's concentration on his family history was an East Coast thing.

Moving between the coasts a few times has taught me about the way works of art, like people, might have different stature in different social settings. In the 1980s it was a story of two Roberts. Among young poets and academics in Boston, Robert Duncan was a little-read, peculiar figure on the outskirts of attention, while Robert Lowell was a major artist, his work a central, commanding presence. For the young poets in

Berkeley, and for my colleagues in the English Department there, Duncan's writing was a vital achievement at the center of living poetry. I remember Duncan stalking through a hallway in Berkeley's Wheeler Hall to visit someone's class, wearing a cape, like the superhero he was in that place and time.

East and West, I missed out on some good things because of the shyness or arrogance, or whatever it was, that kept me from ever completely joining the life of either Boston or the Bay Area. In Berkeley, I witnessed my social group's devotion to good food, natural fibers, elegant sporting goods and hikes in Wildcat Canyon—a consumer paradise that brought out the skeptical, New Jersey sourpuss in me, even as I took pleasure in the food and the scenery.

In a mild, privileged way I was a Kirk Pettiford on either coast, an outsider with a discordant knack for certain things. It could be that my origins were too remote in spirit from both Cambridge and Berkeley. I try to comfort myself with one of the first things Homer tells about the most human of all the heroes, in the first lines of the *Odyssey*: "He saw the cities of many peoples and he learnt their ways." Unheroic, but something to aspire to, I tell myself. I treasure the poet Tony Hoagland's words in a review of my first book: "What has six arms, an enormous appetite, and roams over the earth devouring experience with omnivorous reverence? The poet Robert Pinsky, that's who." I cling to the idea of "omnivorous reverence" and to the verb "roams."

Or maybe that's a rationalization for what I missed by not getting the apprenticeship of attachment to an older poet in the generation of John Ashbery, Robert Duncan, Allen Ginsberg, Robert Lowell, James Merrill, Sylvia Plath, Adrienne Rich—in other words, the contemporary poetry of those days. I read poems by those living seniors, but never as their devoted student in the way I was a devoted student-as-reader of the earlier Modernist generation of T. S. Eliot, Marianne

Moore, Wallace Stevens, William Carlos Williams, H.D. and Ezra Pound. Whether Pound would like it or not, he was now my Ezra Pound, my flawed but vital teacher.

I had read Williams's statement that when he was young he memorized Francis Turner Palgrave's old-fashioned *The Golden Treasury*, a large, popular anthology of historical poetry. Williams's memory of that early attachment made me feel better about my efforts to study as an apprentice of dead poets from Fulke Greville and George Gascoigne to Emily Dickinson and Walt Whitman. Whatever the terms mean, I was more interested in "poetry" than I was in "contemporary poetry."

When people heard I was working on a book about contemporary poetry, I remember questions like, "Will there be a chapter on the Confessionals?" Um, no. "On the Beats?" Well, it's not that kind of book. "Chapters on Dickey, Plath, Berryman, Bishop, Olson?" No.

I could see from the person's face a gradual conclusion that I wasn't really writing a book, just pretending. When I finished *The Situation of Poetry* I resisted the publisher's urging to re-title it something snappy like *Poetry Now* or *Poetry Today*. The book makes unlikely pairings, comparing Allen Ginsberg with George Gascoigne, Sylvia Plath with John Clare, Frank Bidart with J. V. Cunningham, Louise Bogan with Frank O'Hara. The single poem with the most pages is Keats's "Ode to a Nightingale." (Second most, James McMichael's "Itinerary.") If I were a thirty-year-old writing the book today I might compare the feeling of "wonder" as a noun in poems by Danez Smith and Ben Jonson. I write about Lowell not as "confessional" but in relation to quoting and dramatic monologues.

For my poet friends in Cambridge, Lowell's central importance was embodied by his Office Hours—the initial caps seem right for those unique sessions he ran in a seminar room at Harvard. That weekly event was an erratic writing work-shop, with interjected lectures. About thirty people, many of them Office Hours regulars, most of them not actual Harvard students, sat at a big central table or in chairs around the room's perimeter. Each week, various people brought photocopies of a poem they had written. After an awkward pause one of those people, maybe someone chosen by Lowell but sometimes a confident soul volunteering spontaneously, would hand out copies of their poem.

I did not live in Cambridge but in subsidized housing for married faculty at Wellesley College, out in the suburbs. With a full teaching schedule and three children, I could not have gotten into town for those peculiar séances if I wanted to—which I did not. But one semester when I was on leave from Wellesley, just back from a year in London and not yet teaching, I did attend two or three times.

It was impressive to hear Lowell responding with his daffy insight, often allusive, to those photocopied poems. Some-times well-known poets who had published books brought their new work to the Office Hours, with Lowell in a dou-ble role as peer and master. He managed that duality with his habit of drifting to enlarge any question or example. I respected how he would bring up unexpected comparisons to William Blake or to Edna St. Vincent Millay—all in his pecu-liar accent, sort of quasi-Southern, a unique personal inven-tion. Somebody told me the fabricated drawl was Lowell's way to disavow Boston by resisting its manner of speaking.

At one of the sessions I attended, encouraged by my friends, I brought in a poem, and Lowell praised it. What he said I can't remember precisely, but I'm sure he wove my poem into his endless, thrilling and obsessive ruminations about poetry. Nothing was more important than the art and its history. In conversation he might at any moment erupt into an interrogation:

"Where is Alexander Pope's best writing, do you think?"

And then, while you were still fumbling for an answer:

"Many people might say the 'Essay on Criticism,' written when he was practically a teenager, but politicians and everybody else are always quoting the 'Essay on Man.'"

My other memory from those visits to the Office Hours was a moment when I disagreed with Lowell. It wasn't as bad as my saying, "I'm surprised at your ignorance," to Mr. Kolibas back in the eighth grade, or the high school duel with Mr. Pulaski. Whatever I said was more like, "I disagree" or "I think you're wrong about that." What I remember is not anything Lowell said next, but a kind of choral gasp from the room as a whole. I was breaking a rule.

Lowell himself more or less shrugged. For all his eccentricities—famously abundant—Lowell had class. My guess is, he was amused by the absurdity of the mouthy, overconfident young Wellesley professor, by the audible shock of his own followers at that reckless dissent, and by his own boredom while presiding over the moment. He later wrote an excellent blurb for *Sadness And Happiness*, my first book of poetry, even though he knew I did not admire his work intensely, the way Frank, Lloyd, Gail and many others did. Maybe he taught me a lesson that Mr. Pulaski had not, and I was still too raw and silly to get it.

Lowell could be funny in a digressive, absurdist way. Somebody's poem reminded him of the time Julius Caesar stopped his entourage outside the house of Cicero so the two of them could chat about literature. The horses and soldiers and palanquins and sycophants waited in the street while inside Cicero's place Caesar and his frequent opponent talked about writing. Lowell described the scene in that peculiar drawl-without-a-region, pinwheel eyes behind his glasses, with no transition between scholarship and goofy riffs. I remember how he threw in the name of a contemporary rival:

"And so Caesar and Cicero talked while all the nobodies waited outside. The two of them chatted—you know, they chatted about good prose and about oratory, and about the writers and politicians they both knew. They gossiped about Jim Dickey."

For me, the West Coast alternative to Lowell was not Robert Duncan but Yvor Winters, my teacher at Stanford in the years between Rutgers and the days of Wellesley College and the Lowell Office Hours. When I went to California that first time, the farthest west I had been was Flemington, New Jersey. I had only a vague idea who Winters was. I knew his reputation as a rigid, conservative academic, a stiff and graceless prig. Shortly after arriving in Palo Alto, before meeting Winters or taking a class with him, I read his essay "Robert Frost: The Spiritual Drifter as Poet."

"And fuck you very much!" I said to the book. I actually threw it across the room. The essay was a dismantling of Frost's philosophical evasions, his hints and feints toward the Emersonian thinking that Winters considered a fatally sloppy, anti-intellectual current in American culture. Even while praising Wallace Stevens or Mina Loy as great poets, he called attention to defects in their ideas.

His customary line was that he had read every poem by every poet of any reputation who wrote in English, and had made his own judgments. If you wanted to disagree with him, you ought to do the same. He and Lowell both had a total, undiluted concentration on poetry—nothing was more important, for either of them. For them, poetry meant the entire, monumental history of the art, not just the mere local neighborhood in time of their contemporaries. Thanks to Winters, I learned to read the sixteenth and seventeenth century poets whose work I love. George Gascoigne's longish poem "Gascoigne's Woodmanship," with the poet's account of his failures and sincerities, moved me.

Even while throwing his book across the room, I was surprised by the subversive, comical grace of Winters's prose. His sentences with their outrageous opinions and poses were light on their feet in a way that reminded me of Oliver Hardy dancing with defiantly ironic elegance, the fat man possibly a better hoofer than Stan Laurel, in their duets. Unlike Hardy, Winters could be vicious as well as nimble:

The only important difference between a chimpanzee and a professor of English is that the professor has a greater command of language. The professor may think himself more handsome, but the chimp thinks otherwise, and the chimp is beyond argument the better athlete. The chimp, of course, would not admit the one kind of superiority which belongs to the professor, because he does not know what it is. The only important difference between the professor and a distinguished poet is that the poet has a greater command of language; but few professors will admit this difference, because almost none understand the nature of the difference—it is for this reason that nearly all are so feeble when they come to the defense of their profession.

He was a dominant figure within his Palo Alto corral in a way completely different from Lowell's centrality in Cambridge. Lowell was an eccentric magnet. Winters was a relentless dictator. He imposed his often crazy literary opinions onto his Stanford disciples, known as the Wintersians, and they saluted. I can remember arguing in his seminar, in defiance of the Wintersian line, that William Butler Yeats was a better poet than T. Sturge Moore. Winters had said the opposite. The disciples in the room smirked at my error.

But I learned more about poetry from Yvor Winters than from any other teacher. And he allowed me a role a bit like that of Fool in a Shakespeare play. He would sometimes say, after a cogent ten or fifteen minutes he had used to demolish some great poet's work, "Mr. Pinsky will now say a few words on behalf of Whitman," or whoever was the victim of the day. I always took the bait, if that is what it was.

Winters as a young man had been the town schoolteacher in Madrid, New Mexico, a small mining community back then, with the town's name pronounced with a stress on the flat *a* of the first syllable, as he explained to us graduate student poets. Besides the academic subjects, he also taught the Madrid children the art of boxing, in which he considered himself an expert.

This was the year of the first bout between heavyweight champion Sonny Liston and the young loudmouth known then as Cassius Clay. The heavyweight boxing championship, in those days, was still the most significant and respected title in sports.

In class the week before the fight, Winters chuckled about it. I remember his exact words:

"Liston is going to make mincemeat out of him."

I didn't know much about boxing, though I had watched the *Friday Night Fights* on TV with my father, who like his own father was a great fan. I should have remembered my father's praise for Sugar Ray Robinson, and his explanation that Robinson's skill as a tap dancer was related to his supremacy as a boxer. "It's all in how you move," I can hear my father saying, words that might have given me insight into the abilities of the future Muhammad Ali, but in Palo Alto I wasn't thinking about my father. His father, my Zaydee Pop, had fought in the professional ring. For my birthdays, he always gave me a pair of boxing gloves. Still, I didn't know much about the sport, and I had no insight into the match

But I knew my role in the Winters circle.

"I think Clay is going to win," I said.

February 25, 1964, was a Tuesday. I went to the Wednesday class—it was so small it met in Winters's office—in a perky mood.

"Mr. Winters," I said. "Did you listen to the fight? Did you enjoy it?"

He laughed, and with a rare smile, maybe even a grin, he gave me an excellent answer. Maybe he had prepared it, but he was also, contrary to his reputation, a good improviser.

"Well," he said, "all the experts were wrong. So this proves I'm an expert."

A year before, I had noticed that Winters was wearing a black armband—the customary sign of bereavement for his generation. A family death of some kind, I assumed, until somebody explained to me that he began wearing the armband after four young girls were killed by the bombing on September 15, 1963, of the Sixteenth Street Baptist Church in Birmingham, Alabama. The armband made me remember that when I arrived at Stanford in 1962 I had posted on the English Department bulletin board an appeal for money to help pay legal costs for my Rutgers classmate Donnie Harris, who was one of a group arrested in the course of voter registration work in Jackson, Mississippi. I wound up sending just two small checks, my own and one from Yvor Winters. The two picture frames that hung on the walls of his mostly undecorated office held a citation from the NAACP and a portrait of Herman Melville.

Browsing issues of *Poetry* in the Stanford library, I came across an April 1961 prose piece by Robert Lowell titled "Yvor Winters: A Tribute." Lowell wrote that Winters's poems "have compassion, and are made of iron . . . They pass Housman's test for true poetry—if I remembered them while shaving, I would cut myself."

Reading Lowell's words there in California, I was impressed by his generosity toward an older artist so distant in way of writing as well as geography. Again, as when he declined Lyndon Johnson's invitation to a reception at the White House and instead marched on the Pentagon with Allen Ginsberg, Robert Lowell showed class.

"Winters likes to declare himself a conservative," Lowell writes in that tribute. "Dim-wits have called him a conservative. He was the kind of conservative who was so original and radical that his poems were never reprinted in the anthologies for almost twenty years . . . a stylist whose diction and metric exemplify two hundred years of American culture."

Winters and Lowell both had their bizarre flaws, larger than normal—as their gifts, too, were larger than normal. I feel about both of them what Winters says about his friend Hart Crane, in the conclusion to his essay "The Significance of *The Bridge* by Hart Crane, Or, What Are We to Think of Professor X?":

> In spite of popular and even academic prejudices to the contrary, it takes a very highly developed intelligence to write great poetry, even a little of it. So far as I am concerned, I would gladly emulate Odysseus, if I could, and go down to the shadows for another hour's conversation with Crane on the subject of poetry; whereas, politeness permitting, I seldom go out of my way to discuss poetry with Professor X.

I would gladly go down to the shadows for another hour's conversation with Winters or Lowell on the subject of poetry.

XIV

A Hat Like That

MARRIED YOUNG, but for a few years before that I did have the social life of a single person. One Friday night, a beautiful young woman and I were standing in the alley outside a club. We watched a young Orthodox Jew emerge from around the corner and walk past us. He was wearing the traditional ankle-length black overcoat and the fur hat called a shtreimel, the shape of a marshmallow but black, and nearly as wide as his shoulders. After he turned the corner, my date smiled at me and said:

"How come you don't wear a hat like that?"

I told her that when the souls of Jewish men are waiting to be reborn the angel in charge asks each one of us, which would we rather have—a splendid mink shtreimel or excellent sexual equipment? And my soul, I explained, had a hat like that last time.

"Your soul," said Ellen Bailey, "never had a hat like that."

This remark about my soul and the guy's hat is a landmark moment in what became our long marriage. She had the wit to see through my blather, and to intuit my fearful worldly aspirations.

The man's fur shtreimel presented to the world an extreme of social and religious affiliation, stronger and more lasting than the group loyalties of the Wintersians, or of MFA students who become devotees of one senior poet or another.

For the "Wintersians" in the Stanford Ph.D. or M.A. programs, the idea seemed to be not necessarily to write like Winters, but to absorb his principles and his tastes, as doctrine. Not me. I respected his writing—I still have by heart his poem "A Summer Commentary" ("Amid the rubble, the fallen fruit / Fermenting in its rich decay, / Smears brandy on the trampling boot")— but with no urge to emulation. Stanford was not like the possibly exaggerated accounts of the University of Iowa MFA program's faculty coteries, and I was not a Wintersian.

Sadness And Happiness, my first book of poems, has its peculiarities: the deliberately corny or deadpan title; the nine-page title poem with its Roman numerals in the middle of sentences; the first poem entitled "Poem About People"; the long final poem entitled "Essay on Psychiatrists"; frequently changing the subject; lurching between rudeness and good manners. Like my homespun baloney about not wearing a shtreimel, everything about the book still feels to me completely like myself, good or bad or some of each.

Social and antisocial, the title poem "Sadness And Happiness" felt like a breakthrough in its urgent inward babble or ecstatic, chatty shpritzing. I see in it a true record of my deepest, most jumbled affiliations. On the one hand, it is organized symmetrically in twelve sections, and in each section five stanzas of four lines each. But on the other hand, the poem streams or screams across the section divisions with its disobedient monologue, a self-preoccupied rant against self-preoccupation. The Roman numerals an orderly parody of order. Literary affiliations? To my ear, the poem aspires to some jangly, unlikely fusion—maybe the propulsion of Allen

Ginsberg but in the tradition of George Gascoigne and the resisted model of William Butler Yeats. Whatever else it does, the poem tells my story in my way:

> A girl touched my sleeve, once,
> held it, deep-eyed; life too at times
> has come up, looked into my face,
> *My Lord, how like you this?* And I?
>
> Always distracted by some secret
> movie camera or absurd audience
> eager for clichés, *Ivanhoe*, de blues,
> *Young Man with a Horn*, the star
>
> tripping over his lance, quill, phallic
> symbol or saxophone—miserable,
> these absurd memories of failure
> to see anything but oneself,
>
> my pride, my consciousness, my shame, my
> sickly haze of Romance—sick too
> the root of joy? "Bale" and "bliss" merge
> in a Petrarchist grin, that sleeve's burden
>
> III
> or chivalric trophy to bear as
> emblem or mark of the holy
> idiot: know ye, this natural stood
> posing amiss while the best prizes
>
> of life bounced off his vague
> pate or streamed between his legs—
> did Korsh, Old Russia's bedlam-sage,
> enjoy having princesses visit his cell?

Would they dote on me as I shake out
a match, my fountain pen in the same
hand, freckling my dim brow with ink?
Into his muttered babble they read tips

on the market, court, marriage—I too
mutter: *Fool, fool!* or *Death!*
or *Joy!* Well, somewhere in the mind's mess
feelings are genuine, someone's

mad voice undistracted, clarity
maybe of motive and precise need
like an enamelled sky, cool
blue of Indian Summer, happiness

IV
like the sex-drowsy saxophones
rolling flatted thirds of the blues
over and over, rocking the dulcet
rhythms of regret, Black music

which tumbles loss over in the mouth
like a moist bone full of marrow . . .

When Princeton University Press, in the first year of its poetry series, accepted this peculiar, self-lamenting book about failure and ebullience, talking to yourself—out loud—as a way out of yourself, I was happily surprised.

Having failed to publish a book of my poems, after many tries, until my early thirties, I had been consciously schooling myself to live a good life as an unpublished poet, without bitterness. Then, *Sadness And Happiness* was selected for three different first-book competitions. I chose Princeton, the reviews were good, and with *The Situation of Poetry* coming out a year later, I went quickly from my internal story—of the middle-aged poet bracing against bitterness—to an external perception by other people (equally a fabrication)—of a new young presence bursting onto the scene.

I was sociable and I was antisocial. My friends of the Lowell sessions at Harvard were also regulars at the Grolier Poetry Book Shop on Plympton Street, fond of its patriarchal owner, the legendary Gordon Cairnie. Not me. For years, the cramped, dark space of the Grolier intimidated me like a club where I was not a member. Cairnie was a grumpy, snobbish presence, not a friendly retailer of the kind I knew how to like.

When I needed a particular book, I would drive to Cambridge from Wellesley, park at a meter, walk right to the Grolier, buy the book, and leave the store with plenty of time left on the meter. I still have ancient copies of books by Louise Bogan and Jack Gilbert I got on those quick, browsing-free visits to the store. I remember the dusty sofa, occupied by Harvard boys wearing cowboy hats and discussing the poetry of Charles Olson while eating hamburgers from McDonald's. After Gordon Cairnie died, a young woman took over the store. Louisa Solano, to my silent applause, got rid of the couch.

But those Harvard kids who sat on the Grolier couch— maybe some of them grew up to be poets I admire, or friends. But I associated them (crazily) with people who bonded as children at sleepover camp in the summer. Growing up in a seashore resort town, on Rockwell Avenue, I didn't know anybody who went to sleepover camp. Or in a reversal, had I been too much like "summer people" in relation to Berkeley and Cambridge?

In the Wellesley years, the poet teaching at MIT, Barry Spacks, organized a group that met once a week. Barry, Frank Bidart, David Ferry, Joyce Peseroff and I got together over wine to discuss poems. Because I had small children, we met at my house, which made me feel a bit like the host. In that spirit, a couple of times when there wasn't much new work to discuss, to fill the gap I presented work I had abandoned or doubted—including what became the title poem of *Sadness And Happiness*. The group convinced me there was something good in it.

I wasn't the only one who benefited from our gatherings. David had not been writing for a few years, and I think the group meetings helped end his dry spell. Joyce was the youngest of us and the only woman, also the only one who had attended an MFA program, having just arrived from UC Irvine, where she had studied with James McMichael. Joyce brought to us one night what became the wonderful title poem of her first book, "The Hardness Scale." Barry Spacks had already published many books. I often quote phrases from Barry's poems to myself, such as his " 'Me!' 'Me!' for the glockenspiel," to voice the normal selfishness of children, and his simile about certain college freshmen. They are like "the swinging door / to the opera just before / the Marx Brothers break through."

Frank Bidart and I became close friends. For my *Inferno* translation, we had hours-long phone consultations about each canto. Though Frank had no Italian, he read several other English translations, prose and verse. Any passage that seemed more clear or interesting to him in another version, he pressed me to change. *The Inferno of Dante* is dedicated to him.

Frank was a Californian, from the prominent Basque family of Central Valley ranches and Bidart Brothers potatoes. I had never known anyone who drove a Porsche until I met Frank. He was in the process of buying a condominium just off Cambridge's elegant Brattle Street, and he received rent every month from a liquor store on Bidart property in

Bakersfield—all part of a history he was determined to reject. Frank for years was a kind of uncle to my kids. Thanks to him, they were the first in their school to have a Nintendo. At Harvard, Frank had befriended Robert Lowell and Elizabeth Bishop, becoming an important helper to both of them. A few times he brought drafts of theirs to share at a meeting of our poetry group.

The group could claim to belong in an ancient tradition— Ben Jonson and his friends reading poems to one another at the Mermaid Tavern, or in Asian cultures, the scholarly elegance of imperial courtiers and statesmen composing poems about friendship, exile and duty—a pre-modern, pre-industrial approach to the art.

In Berkeley, when Bob Hass was teaching at St. Mary's College and Louise Glück was a visiting writer at the university, the three of us used to meet in a way similar to the Barry Spacks nights in Wellesley. One time, we tailored assignments for one another. Bob had to write an explicitly Roman Catholic poem, and Louise had to write a poem that was funny. My assignment was to write one that stayed with one subject and image, without hopping around. (Louise's poem was about a conversation between Bob and me.)

But the antisocial element also drove "Sadness And Happiness." The poem's grungy parade through Central Square; the two abstractions of the title; the rushing, crowded sentences; the allusions to Yeats and Ellington. All came from inside. But "Sadness And Happiness" also relishes its outward, negative, conscious resistance to other kinds of poetry: on one side, the metrical Wintersian mode with rhymes on "skill/dust, will/trust"; and on the other side, the orphic, Jungian-elemental mode with primal nouns like "blood," "stone" and "earth." A yacking voice partly borrowed from Ginsberg sets the poem's climactic scene in the opposite of Harvard Square, with the opposite of chamber music:

Central Square suddenly become
the most strange of places

as a Salvation Army band marches
down the middle, shouldering aside
the farting, evil-tempered traffic,
brass pitting its triplets and sixteenths

into the sundown fray of cops, gesturing
derelicts, young girls begging quarters,
shoppers and released secretaries, scruffy
workers and students, dropouts, children

whistling, gathering as the band
steps in place tootling and rumbling
in the square now, under an apocalypse
of green-and-pink sky, with paper

and filth spinning in the wind, crazy,
everyone—band, audience, city, lady
trumpeter fiddling spit-valve, John
Philip Sousa, me, Christianity, crazy

VII
and all empty except for you,
who look sometimes like a stranger . . .

The "you"—the exception that begins section VII—is for me, and possibly but not necessarily for the reader, the singular person who beholds the soul that wears no hat of affiliation.

I used to hear a reasonable question: "Does raising a family take away time and energy from your writing?" Years later, I read the words of Justice Ruth Bader Ginsberg, who said, about raising her daughter while in law school, "each part of my life gave me respite from the other." I recognize the idea. Living with my family freed me from spending much energy hunting for other people. There were funny, unpredictable people available for company, under the same roof. There may be some evasive bravado to that statement. One way or another, I was choosing to walk alone as a writer—sometimes, pushing a baby carriage. A pretty mild way to be an outlier, but still, in the social world of MFA programs that's what I was.

A funny poem by Theodore Roethke begins, "It wasn't Ernest; it wasn't Scott— / The boys I knew when I went to pot." Roethke writes about becoming a poet in the bars where he "learned a lot / In Ecorse, Toledo, and Wyandotte." My approximation of Roethke's not hanging out with Hemingway and Fitzgerald in Paris might be my not talking with other young poets, in some Soho or Brooklyn or Iowa City gathering place, about a new book by John Ashbery or Adrienne Rich. I read the work of those poets, but I was also, in my social life, learning to value the poetry of Edward Lear, Dr. Seuss, and Walter de la Mare.

George Gascoigne dedicates his poem "Gascoigne's Woodmanship" to his rich, titled patron. The poem is a prolonged defense of the poet's failures in many pursuits, as being earnest but lacking in worldly guile and shrewd corruptions. The concluding example is from being on a hunt with the noble patron and failing to hit anything: inept woodmanship. So Gascoigne then imagines—he *tells* us that it is an imagining—that he has mistakenly, even more ineptly, against the rules, killed a nursing mother deer with his arrow:

> Let me imagine in this worthless verse,
> If right before me, at my standing's foot
> There stood a doe, and I should strike her dead,
> And then she prove a carrion carcass too,
> What figure might I find within my head,
> To 'scuse the rage which ruled me so to do?

Having imagined his mistake, he dares to go further, recklessly, into the conscious and explicit mode, to actually "interpret" his own imagining of the deer he shot in his error. Bad luck, bad woodmanship. Or, a divine message:

> Some might interpret with plain paraphrase,
> That lack of skill or fortune led the chance,
> But I must otherwise expound the case;
> I say Jehovah did this doe advance . . .

Jehovah sent the doe into his imagination, says Gascoigne, to teach him the shrewd, worldly arts of skepticism, compromise and flattery:

> . . . and made her bold to stand before me so,
> Till I had thrust mine arrow to her heart,
> That by the sudden of her overthrow
> I might endeavor to amend my part
> And turn mine eyes that they no more behold
> Such guileful marks as seem more than they be:
> And though they glister outwardly like gold,
> Are inwardly like brass, as men may see:
> And when I see the milk hang in her teat,
> Methinks it saith, old babe, now learn to suck,
> Who in thy youth couldst never learn the feat
> To hit the whites which live with all good luck.
> Thus have I told my Lord (God grant in season)
> A tedious tale in rhyme, but little reason.

I love how he combines the eloquence of "by the sudden of her overthrow" with the startling, words-of-one-syllable immediacy of "old babe, now learn to suck."

The final lines of "Sadness And Happiness" acknowledge "Gascoigne's Woodmanship" among my inspiring models. The conclusion also credits family life as the source of the unpoetic (as some would call it) title, "Sadness And Happiness":

> . . . old coaches and teachers, everyone
> I ever knew) cheering louder as I tip
>
> XII
> my imaginary, ironic hat and blow
> false kisses crossing home, happiness
> impure and oddly memorable as the sad
> agony of recalled errors lived over
>
> before sleep, poor throws awry
> or the ball streaming through,
> between my poor foolish legs, crouching
> amazed like a sot. Sport—woodmanship,
>
> ball games, court games—has its cruel
> finitude of skill, good-and-bad, as does
> the bizarre art of words: confirmation
> of a good word, *polvo*, dust, reddish gray
>
> powder of the ballfield, *el polvo*
> rising in pale puffs to glaze lightly
> the brown ankles and brown bare feet in
> Cervantes' poem of the girl dancing, all
>
> dust now, poet, girl. It is intolerable
> to think of my daughters, too, dust—
> *el polvo*—or you whose invented game,
> Sadness and Happiness, soothes them
>
> XIII
> to sleep: can you tell me one sad
> thing that happened today, Can you think

of one happy thing to tell me that
happened to you today, organizing

life—not you too dust like the poets,
dancers, athletes, their dear skills
and the alleged glittering gaiety of
Art which, in my crabwise scribbling hand,

no less than Earth the change of all
changes breedeth, art and life
both inconstant mothers, in whose
fixed cold bosoms we lie fixed,

desperate to devise anything, any
sadness or happiness, only
to escape the clasped coffinworm
truth of eternal art or marmoreal

infinite nature, twin stiff
destined measures both manifested
by my shoes, coated with dust or dew which no
earthly measure will survive.

XV

Magic Mountain

I N 1977, a week or two after Robert Lowell died, I was reading one of his books on an airplane. The passenger next to me was a pilot from a different airline, in a courtesy seat on the way to his next assignment, he explained. He asked me about my book, and when I showed him the author's name, he said:

"Didn't I just read something about him in the paper?"

"Well, he died last week. Maybe you saw an obituary."

"Yes, that's it. He seemed like somebody who should've been famous."

"Famous" is relative. The pilot was on the borderlands of those who might apply the word to Robert Lowell. "Famous" is also a matter of degree. I have been asked:

"Grandpa, are you famous?"

"Only a little bit."

"Fame is a fickle food," writes Emily Dickinson, "upon a shifting plate." The word "fame," she suggests, has a sleazy undertone. When the pilot and I had that conversation about Lowell, I remembered a saying of the Roman politician and writer Cato the Elder. He said he'd rather have people ask why there was no statue of him in Rome, than why there was one.

Fame varies over time. For decades, the two most important kinds of performer in the U.S. were: bandleader and crooner. One person stood out as the most successful at filling both roles. Vaughn Monroe (1911–1973) as a bandleader and crooner, was in a class by himself. On Saturday nights, NBC Radio broadcast Monroe singing with his band, in live performances from a different college campus every week. His records sold in the millions. Tall and handsome, Monroe appeared in movies and on television.

He had an unusual hit song, "Riders in the Sky," a minor-key, up-tempo cowboy ballad about "ghost riders" galloping high up in the storm clouds, "chasing the devil's herd," as he sang in his deep voice. When I was in elementary school, many of us kids knew the lyrics, about the "mighty herd of red-eyed cows . . . a-plowin' through the ragged skies, and up a cloudy draw," and the spooky refrain, "Yi-pi-yi-ay, yi-pi-yi-o." Our parents danced to Monroe's music, including hits like his "Racing with the Moon." Vaughn Monroe was at a pinnacle of fame.

Also born in 1911, a few months before Vaughn Monroe, was Elizabeth Bishop, today possibly the most celebrated and widely read American poet of her generation. During her lifetime, Bishop was admired, but with a sometimes condescending note of praise for her "good eye," consigning her to the category "woman poet." Along with refusing to have her work included in anthologies of poetry by women, Bishop felt that in some ways she was not taken quite as seriously as her male poet friends John Berryman, Randall Jarrell and Robert Lowell.

The wheel turns. At the moment I am typing these words, many thousands of people around the world are reading poems by Elizabeth Bishop, such as "One Art," and "At the

Fishhouses." Hundreds of thousands, possibly more, would recognize her name. They may be quoting her work or discussing it on Facebook or Twitter. Only a handful of scholarly souls interested in the 1940s and 1950s are thinking about Vaughn Monroe and his music.

Terms for Bishop's enduring reputation might be "vertical fame" compared to the singing bandleader's "horizontal fame." I don't mean to diminish Vaughn Monroe, or the reputation he enjoyed, as a "fickle food," as Emily Dickinson puts it, upon the "shifting plate" of his radio show, his university appearances, and "Riders in the Sky," which I had by heart in grade school.

Poets think about such things. In his 1975 poem "A Magic Mountain," Czesław Miłosz considers the idea of his own fame:

> So I won't have power, won't save the world?
> Fame will pass me by, no tiara, no crown?
> Did I then train myself, myself the Unique,
> To compose stanzas for gulls and sea haze,
> To listen to the foghorns blaring down below?

The title alludes to the sequestered asylum of Thomas Mann's novel, but the Magic Mountain of the poem is Berkeley itself, the Bay Area with its absence of real seasons—and by implication, Berkeley's apparent freedom from the historical agonies of Europe. Miłosz quotes a Russian-born Berkeley colleague about their fatally bland new setting on the Bay: "Where so little changes you hardly notice how time goes by. / This is, you will see, a magic mountain." In the temperate present tense of California, fame had passed by the exiled Professor Miłosz, whose name did not appear in the tormented, false and tyrannized official histories of Polish poetry. No tiara for him, no crown. Not even a mention in the official encyclopedia.

In 1980, my first year in Berkeley, Bob Hass and I had set a September date to meet with Miłosz so we could discuss working with him on English versions of his poetry. A possibility, I felt, to enlarge my own writing as part of the move from East Coast to West, to collaborate with two poets I admired, one a good friend from Stanford days and the other from a different language and an earlier generation.

But a faculty meeting at St. Mary's College came up for Bob, so we had to cancel. We picked a new day about a week later. Then I had to cancel that second date—and before we could reschedule, the newspaper stories appeared. Czesław Miłosz had been awarded the Nobel Prize in Literature. A crown, a tiara.

The crown coincided with a statue—not in Cato's Rome, exactly, but lines from a poem by Miłosz were inscribed on the monument in Gdansk commemorating the uprising that unified Polish workers and students in the Solidarity movement. "Fame," in the phrase of his poem, had not "passed him by," after all.

For Hass and me, the Nobel news included a half-serious "Oh shit" element. Those two appointments we had canceled made it feel awkward to ask Czesław for a new appointment—as though only now did we have time for him. Might we never work with the older poet we admired? Eventually, the meeting took place and Bob and I began making English versions from literal trots provided by Miłosz and Renata Gorczynski. They were the two bilingual members of a group Miłosz suggested naming after the poet's Berkeley address on Grizzly Peak Boulevard. Grisleigh Peake, he mused, could be the pseudonymous author of any published translations.

I remember Elizabeth Bishop complaining about the reprinted copies of her poem "The Fish" she would see posted in many bait-and-tackle shops: pirated editions, she said, violations of copyright, with her not getting a nickel from them. Thom Gunn said that whenever he saw his poem "Night Taxi" posted in a cab, he felt flattered. Two apparently opposite responses, but again the same wry sense of recognition and the imperfections of that shifting plate.

In Berkeley, Czesław could take sardonic pleasure in a Polish newspaper photograph of people lined up for a block, around the corner from a bookstore in Warsaw, where the Soviet regime had banned his name for decades. The people in the picture were queued up waiting to buy the authorized, quickly produced, government-approved edition of his poetry.

Miłosz in his seventies laughed at that picture in a way that bewildered me a little, back then in my early forties. It took me a while to understand how the candid pleasure of a stroked ego might blend with a skeptical amusement at worldly shallowness. Public acclaim, like public neglect, reflected mindless currents tangential to art, along with art itself. A European poet thirty years older than me was demonstrating his fatalistic, undeluded understanding of public attention that he enjoyed.

One day, I came home to see Miłosz sitting on the living room sofa. My daughter had let him in, explaining that I was on my way home. I had thought he was still away from Berkeley, on a trip to Poland and Italy. I sat down next to him and he showed me a new poem in typescript. It was one of the English trots that Renata and Czesław would create, for Bob and me to try refining the poem's idiom and rhythm. The new poem that day was in sections, three or four typed pages in Czesław's clear but hasty English. He asked me the usual question for such moments between poets:

"What do you think?"

I began to stall and mumble, not understanding some of what I had just read. Maybe I tried to specify a passage I wasn't clear about. Whatever I said, Czesław responded with a remarkable sentence.

"The Pope," he said, laughing at his own argument by authority, but also meaning it, "likes this poem very much."

Pope John Paul II was Polish. As Karol Józef Wojtyła, a devout young man who wrote poetry, the future Pope would think of Czesław Miłosz, already an admired literary figure, ten years older than Wojtyła himself, as famous. My sketchy knowledge of that history did not help me know what to say next, about a supremely eminent authority liking Czesław's poem.

A few years ago, visiting a very good liberal arts college, I met with a class of English majors. Trying to be helpful, I explained to them that in a poem quoting "Julius Marx," I was referring to Groucho: Julius was his birth name. Through the haze that can come with being a Distinguished Guest I detected a blank.

"Groucho Marx," I said to that room of high-achieving Americans in their late teens or early twenties. "Groucho. You do know who Groucho is, right?"

In a group of maybe thirty students, four or five had some idea of who Groucho was. From their parents or grandparents, I presume. Not one of them had seen so much as a clip from *Horse Feathers* or *Duck Soup*. Julius Marx, born in 1890, was the same age as my grandparents, but for me he was kind of eternal. For these students, he was kind of the same age as me.

Julius ("Groucho") Marx had a mutually admiring exchange of letters with T. S. Eliot. He inspired the anthropomorphic stork that still imitates his voice to market a brand of pickles. He influenced nearly every American comic, past and present, white and Black, male and female, for generations. Most of them could do an impression of him. One of his famous quips, the one about not wanting to be a member of any club that would accept him, was a credo in relation to the white-Protestant-only country clubs and fraternity houses of my youth. Elizabeth Bishop declined to have her work included in anthologies of woman poets, for reasons that went back to the condescending or ghetto-like anthologies of poems by women, books that she recalled from her youth—a variation of the Groucho principle.

But Groucho Marx was not, in the generation of those English majors I talked to, famous. From the magic mountain or provincial time of my own generation, I tried to make a comparison for them by suggesting some figure at the peak for them, some icon of the present moment whose eventual oblivion might shock them someday in the future, when they were my age and talking to college students. The best I could do was Harry Potter or Princess Leia—possibly dated already.

The shifting plate can include locality, as well as publications, movies, hit records, podcasts, electronic media and their successors. Czesław Miłosz did great work while living in the magic mountain of Berkeley, but eventually he left it for Kraków. He felt more at home there.

Berkeley turned out to be a magic mountain for me, too. I learned a lot from the translation work with Czesław and Bob. I wrote the computer entertainment *Mindwheel* and I published my books *History of My Heart* and *The Want Bone*. Two of my three children graduated from Berkeley High. But after ten years I returned to the East Coast, where I felt more at home . . . or, to put it another way, where the passage of time felt more real to me.

Emily Dickinson sought approval, and she did write those lines about fame. But at root, I have concluded, the real masters have above all a total, consuming devotion not to fame or profit or pleasure but, rather—surprisingly, some would say— to difficulty. Fame is a coincidental by-product of what makes certain people crave the bottomless difficulties of their profession or art. Working for excellence becomes addictive, as with a sport or a video game. An infinite difficulty, pursuit of never-complete mastery, can become a supreme need.

When Sandy Koufax, the unsurpassed baseball pitcher, talks about pitching, he does it in the first-person present: "I put my foot on the rubber at *this* angle." Watching a game at Camden Yards, he saw a pitcher I won't name leave the game for a relief pitcher with two outs in the sixth inning. The guy had given up only three earned runs—not a bad outing. He was respected as a good starting pitcher in the American League. But Sandy frowned up at a TV monitor showing a close-up of the man's face.

"Why is he smiling? His team is behind, four to two. And he's smiling? That's why he'll never be any good."

When we were both invited to the White House—it was a reception for notable American Jews—Sandy and I noticed how one of our fellow guests was visibly, totally unimpressed by him, and by me. His line of work and mine equally held no interest for someone invited to the event for having produced an extremely successful kind of figure-enhancing underwear. While our amused wives watched, Sandy tried explaining to the girdle entrepreneur who I was, and I tried explaining who Sandy was. Both failed. Baseball and poetry were equally meaningless on the shifting plate of business, or of fashion, with their different skills and difficulties. Politely, the entrepreneur drifted away.

Writing a good poem is, for poets, the supreme and most desirable difficulty—a difficulty all the more magnetic (and fearsome) because it takes a new, unanticipated form, every time. The fearful, obsessive and addictive sweat of difficulty is the generator.

Cato the Elder, in the saying I like, does not deny that, yes, he *would appreciate* people asking why there was no statue of him in Rome. Even better would be a statue, with everybody appreciating why it was there. Cato does not doubt what he or anyone else has done for Rome. What he doubts is the famous-making power of the institutions and fads, the random committees and tweets and money deals and ulterior politics, that raise the statues.

It's too bad but not tragic that Elizabeth Bishop got more recognition after she died than in her lifetime. She did win prizes. And I believe she would be indifferent to the fame of the most popular American poet ever. His book sold a million copies when that number meant a lot. He had not only a much-syndicated newspaper column and a popular weekly radio program, he even had his own show on NBC television, in the early days of the medium. Edgar Guest (1881–1959), author of *A Heap o' Livin'* and *Just Folks*, was as well-known as Vaughn Monroe.

Elizabeth Bishop would not have coveted the fame of Edgar Guest for one second. Like Miłosz, she courted a higher destiny than sales or prizes. The distance between her art and Guest's popularity is a crucial terrain. In Bishop, I hear plain language of a kind I have heard all my life, deployed as a way to confront mystery. In Guest, I hear an exaggerated affectation of ordinary speech, a calculated appeal to the anti-intellectual by an expert populist entertainer.

In his most famous poem, "A Heap o' Livin'," Guest engineered a rural dialect and misspellings that might be called hyper-real Americana. In a bit of biographical comedy, or yet another score for the immigrant strain in American art, Edgar Guest came from England. Born in the industrial city of Birmingham, he entered the United States as a young Brit at the age of ten, and grew up in Detroit. Maybe he constructed his rustic dialect poems with hints from vaudeville or the movies. He has had his successors, and equivalents in poetry, as in the other arts and in the public life of every period, of course including the present.

The same part of me that imagines President Grant buying whiskey from my grandfather is aware that Mark Twain anticipated and derided Edgar Guest and his "It takes a heap o' livin' in a house t' make it home." Twain made fun of "A Heap o' Livin'" and its admirers long before the poem was written, just as he anticipated and parodied professional wrestling and academic literary fads. While many others were watching the cornball television show of Lawrence Welk, Mark Twain would be tuned in to a different channel, watching Sid Caesar.

Twain created the maudlin young poet Emmeline Grangerford, epitome of American taste in one of its forms. In the same book, he created the revival meetings, Donald Trump rallies and (in effect) reality TV shows staged by his characters the Duke and the Dauphin. *The Adventures of Huckleberry Finn*, in which Emmeline Grangerford's poetry and those two fakers appear, is sometimes banned, while the Duke and the Dauphin are in Congress.

When my daughter Caroline was five or six years old, she used the word "famous" in a conversation with Robert Lowell, who was at our house for some reason I forget. His hair at the time hung down in long, gray strings, mostly at the back.

"You look like somebody famous," Caroline said, to my surprise. Then she added, "Benjamin Franklin."

"He was a terrible man, a very bad man," said Lowell.

Caroline didn't seem to notice that remark. She was still thinking.

"I mean, not like Benjamin Franklin but like a Christmas ornament my friend Heather made out of Play-Doh, that looked like Benjamin Franklin."

That threw Lowell off his stride.

"Well . . . he was a terrible man," he repeated, uncertainly.

XVI

Hyper-Adventures

WAS RAISED in the south of France, in a castle that had been in my family for centuries. One day in my early teens, my tutor told me I was old enough to learn the secret motto of my ancestors. That loyal person responsible for my education took me to a disused part of the castle and led me up a dark stairway to a room I had never seen before. There, on a ceiling-high tapestry lit by a shaft of sunlight, I read the words:

Shorter Hours, Better Pay.

That silly story, to my surprise, was believed, even after the punch line, by one of my Berkeley colleagues, a distinguished scholar with a global reputation. I told it in a discussion about academic jobs and salaries, the kind of thing that used to make the poet James Merrill, a Merrill Lynch heir, politely fall asleep. The academic pecking order that bored Merrill as a multimillionaire repelled me, with my own inheritance from Milford and Sylvia Pinsky and Rockwell Avenue.

In variations of the story, the secret motto might be "Hum a Few Bars and We'll Fake It." Or, instead of the hidden tapestry, the phrase is on the Pinsky coat of arms. It might be a war cry the Pinsky ancestors yelled, whirling their maces as they galloped into battle. In other tellings, the motto inscribed on our shield is the Latin for "All of the Above."

Why do I make these jokes? Most obviously, I guess, in a spirit of social defensiveness and aggression, a traditional American response to being looked on as a hayseed or as an immigrant or a wage slave or an actual slave or a hillbilly or an ethnic outcast. The socially belittled citizen appropriates and mocks the chivalrous past claimed by those who created English Literature. The inside-out tradition ranges back to Twain's Connecticut Yankee, and to Bert Williams, the great Black vaudevillian, singing "Nobody." Generations of Jewish comics found their ways to resist and enter a culture shaped by the majority religion.

The musician's motto "Hum a few bars and we'll fake it" expresses my own habits of mind. Preparation makes me nervous. If a scholar writes to me, inquiring about allusions in "Shirt" or "The Figured Wheel," I need to politely but evasively invoke the spirit of making things up. If the premise can be that one is making it up on the fly, then the standards feel easier to meet. The anxiety creates its own form of preparation,

The phone rang in my office one afternoon in 1981, my first year teaching at UC Berkeley. (My parents always called it "UCLA, Berkeley" with breezy assurance.) The caller said he was Ihor Wolosenko, president of Synapse, a software company.

Back then, I could not have defined "software." Ihor asked me, had I heard of *Zork*.

I had not. *Zork*, he explained, was the dominant product in a field of computer entertainment known as "text adventures"—had I heard of them?

"No."

"It's a kind of game—" Ihor said, "but more than a game, an interactive fiction. You type phrases like 'go north' or 'open door' or 'pick up sword' or 'look at sword,' and more text unravels. In *Zork*, you start off in a nearly empty house. If you try, you discover a trapdoor leading to an immense underground world of demented trolls and so forth. Lots of chambers and hidden passageways. Are you familiar with digital computers? Have you used one?"

"No. Not really."

"Well, you read *Zork* from a computer screen. There's not much in the way of emotion or character, but the reader gets to create the story. At Synapse, we're looking for good *literary* writers to help us create something better than *Zork*. All the appeal of a text adventure, but with more human feeling . . . Do you think you might be interested?"

"Yes," I said. So I wrote a computer game, *Mindwheel*, marketed by Synapse in 1984 as an "Electronic Novel."

About ten years after that "yes" to Ihor Wolosenko, I had a similar conversation with Tod Machover, a composer at MIT's Media Lab. Might I want to write the libretto for an opera? I knew only a little more about operas than I had about text adventures. But like Ihor, Tod suggested that my lack of experience could be an advantage by creating a fresh approach. In other words, hum a few bars and we'll fake it. So I wrote the libretto for *Death and the Powers*, which premiered at the Opéra of Monte Carlo on September 24, 2010.

Mindwheel uses the premise of computer-enabled time travel through immortal minds. *Death and the Powers* is a play-within-a-play staged by onstage, singing robots descended from characters who pursue immortality by uploading their consciousness. My poem "The Robots" reflects some of those preoccupations:

THE ROBOTS

When they choose to take material form they will
 resemble
Dragonflies, not machines. Their wings will shimmer.

Like the chorus of Greek drama they will speak
As many, but in the first person singular.

Their colors in the sky will canopy the surface of the
 earth.
In varying unison and diapason they will dance the
 forgotten.

Their judgment in its pure accuracy will resemble grace
 and in
Their circuits the one form of action will be
 understanding.

Their exquisite sensors will comprehend our very dust
And recreate the best and the worst of us, as though in
 art.

The poem tries to include my admiration for a certain kind
of thought, or for thinking itself as imagined by my Synapse
programmer friends, in their playful fascination with the
mind. its omnivorous quickness and patience, its way of finding underground rivers and hidden corridors between things
that seem unconnected.

    The opera was developed and rehearsed at MIT. There in
the Media Lab I saw the prototype for a prosthetic arm, dou-
ble life-sized, programmed to move its exquisitely articulated
fingers, its wrist and elbow joints, all precisely rotating from
a shoulder in its socket. One of my MIT opera collaborators

had created Kismet, a vast program connected to a rudimentary puppet-face and a baby-like voice. You could converse with Kismet, which was designed to learn language the way human infants do, by listening and interchange. Behind the squeaky voice and moving eyebrows, was an entire floor packed with ultra-powerful mainframe computers. At Synapse, too, people were working on digital understandings of spoken language, refining and supercharging the early psychotherapy programs with their predictable, "Tell me more about that" and "What about your parents?"

Both *Mindwheel* and *Death and the Powers* ramble greedily into the historical past, as well as possible futures. Both projects also gave me a break from familiar categories of work in the English departments where I earned my bread, UC Berkeley in the *Mindwheel* years and Boston University while *Death and the Powers* was created. At Synapse and then at the Media Lab, I was glad to visit a new kind of marketplace. Not the marketplace of money—neither game nor opera was a bonanza of that kind—but a stimulating, messy place of exchange like a downtown, an agora where different kinds of people bustled and gabbled: more like my grandfather's bar than a college campus.

Both collaborations, the opera and the game, also involved compromises. In the libretto for *Death and the Powers* I wrote that the robots should look like dragonflies, an image that survives in "The Robots." In the actual production they looked more like vacuum cleaners. *Mindwheel* was marketed as "an Electronic Novel by Robert Pinsky, Author and Steven Hales & William Mataga, Programmers." The package was a hardcover book, containing the game on disc in an envelope attached to the inside cover, along with many pages of cheesy copy—filler summoned by Ihor from the murky depths of Synapse. For him, the word "novel" added highbrow cachet. But I was thrilled by the challenge of working on a game (the word I preferred) at Synapse's suite of rooms in an El Cerrito office park.

The Synapse "Pit," the space where the programmers worked, resembled an amusement parlor. Weird gadgets appeared, including a prototype omnidirectional rolling device controlling an on-screen cursor—the thing had a wire tail, so it was called a "mouse." One day the mouse broke, so all purposeful work stopped while everybody in the Pit fiddled with it and discussed it, in a state of mind I thought was like the trance of working on a poem. The muse, testing to see if you're a genuine maniac, may show up just when you have a final exam or a meeting about income taxes, or (for those in the Synapse Pit) the day's programming assignments.

With my *Mindwheel* collaborators, I spun the story of our game's second-person quest. At the outset of your adventure, a scientist named Dr. Virgil connects your brain to a supercomputer that enables you, the protagonist-reader, to travel through the terrain of four powerful minds: Dr. Eva Fein, an Einsteinian humanist and scientist; Bobby Clemon, an assassinated, charismatic rock star and radical activist; the Generalissimo, a boastful dictator; and the Poet, a Da Vinci–Shakespeare figure. You must meet challenges and solve puzzles in the setting of these minds, each of them a populated landscape on your quest to reach the wheel-shaped MacGuffin that is your goal.

My programmer coauthors encouraged me to create difficult puzzles. The game customer, they explained, pays for demanding problems, hoping for many hours of fun trying to solve them. So in *Mindwheel*, to free your ally, a bird-woman imprisoned in a cage, you the protagonist-reader must solve a riddle adapted from Walter Raleigh's poem about the cards and dice. In Raleigh's sixteenth century poem, the mystical-sounding, prophetic language of four kings (playing cards) and shaking bones (dice) reaches its finale in the morning, announced by a sunrise herald, a creature "Whose very beard is flesh, and mouth is horn." Only by typing "rooster" or "cock" can the reader advance. Elsewhere in *Mindwheel*, knowing the poetry of Emily Dickinson and Robert Hayden is helpful. (There used to be a niche market for hint-books.)

I supplied the programmers with long tables of what we called "Weather": text hints that drifted into the narrative at a regular pace; and "Drivel": text that might look like "Weather" but had no problem-solving value. For the programmers, a reader's need to tell Weather from Drivel, on the demanding quest for a solution, was one more attractive difficulty.

As consumers of games themselves, Steve and William kept returning to their theme. If you paid money for a game, they said, you wanted it to be enjoyably extensive and many-tunneled. What they said reminded me of my dislike of poetry that presented itself as above all "accessible," and also of poetry that held itself as too cool for meaning. Implicitly, the programmers and I agreed that we loved meaning. The wackier, the more meaningful, and the more difficult, the better.

Many code-writers in the Pit had dropped out of college, or had skipped beginning it. I enjoyed watching those twenty-year-old geniuses get into philosophical discussions about what my Berkeley colleagues would call "narratology." Does a scene (time) take place in a room (space)? Or does the room happen in the scene?

They assigned me to fill in hundreds of noun and verb slots in a "dialogue table." My English Department colleague the poet Peter Scott visited Synapse and tested a prototype of *Mindwheel*. Using the keyboard to speak with a female character, Peter typed, "You look like my mother." The character, recombining bits of text, responded, "I will look any way you want me to look." Peter seemed dazzled by that psychosexual response, and maybe a little shaken.

For my work on *Mindwheel*, Synapse gave me a computer. The brand was Atari. Bulky, with less memory than an entry-level smartphone of a few years later, that 1981 model had a six-inch monochrome monitor. I fell in love with the watery bubble-world of black letters afloat on amber. I poured language into it, as required by the programmers, with the words appearing on the screen with a weightless ease I couldn't attain with a pen or my IBM Selectric typewriter.

For about a year I typed into the Atari everything meant to be read from a screen, while on the Selectric I typed out everything meant to be read from paper. Screen was to paper as Synapse, Inc., was to the University of California: two separate locales for my life in writing, with poetry enveloping both of them.

One day I was having trouble getting started on a book review. The assigned book was the collected prose of Philip Larkin. I was finding it hard to balance my admiration for the English poet's best poems with my revulsion at attitudes he struck in this prose book, with moves calculated to offend conventional liberals like me. Jazz, Larkin wrote, began to decline when Black musicians became less eager to please white audiences. In the most Philistine terms—absurdly, ignoring the popularity and influence of both artists—he said he found the music of Charlie Parker and the pictures of Pablo Picasso off-putting in their perverse difficulty.

Repelled and stalled, I turned to the fluency of the computer's bubble world, less intimidating than harsh white paper and the splendid percussion of the Selectric. I composed the first pages of the Larkin review on the quiet, monochrome Atari. I saved what I had written onto a five-and-a-quarter-inch floppy disc. With the disc I drove to El Cerrito, where a Synapse dot-matrix machine rattled my words onto a scroll of paper. I was now an early adopter of the computer as a tool for what is still called "writing."

As the governing presence of Dr. Virgil suggests, *The Figured Wheel* was not the main literary allusion in the game. I remember one of the play-testers at Synapse, after she had read several review articles in the gamer press, discussing our product, saying, "I've got to read this 'Dante's *Inferno.*' Everybody keeps comparing it to *Mindwheel.*"

XVII

Infernal

I N 1951, when I was eleven, my mother suffered a brain injury, with prolonged effects. She and my father, with my five-year-old sister and our infant brother, were looking at a model home, the builder's sample in a tract of "ranch houses," part of the postwar building boom.

The five of us were living in a two-bedroom, one-bathroom apartment in what was becoming more than ever the wrong part of town—a source of stormy arguments between Milford and Sylvia. Weekend after weekend, they left the apartment to tour houses they couldn't afford. I hated the futility and muffled rage of those expeditions, so I refused to come along, a gloomy eleven-year-old staying home to enjoy some privacy—and the piano.

We got the piano, an Aeolian baby grand, for free from people who advertised it at no charge for anyone willing to move it from their carriage-house studio. They had painted it pea-green, but it was a good piano. For a small fee, our seltzer-delivery man, Mr. Popik, moved the piano on his truck from that carriage house on an estate in Deal to our apartment on Rockwell Avenue.

The house they were inspecting the day my mother fell had an unfinished attic, reached by a folding stairway. At the top, she handed the baby Richard to my father. Then she stepped out between the joists, onto what turned out to be unsupported insulation. On the way down in her fall to the floor below, her head banged into a joist.

At the age of thirty-four, Sylvia Pinsky entered a terrible time for herself and for us, her family: the years of the concussion. She suffered vertigo, severe headaches, nausea, extreme sensitivity to light and sound. Looking down, especially from the top of stairs, made her so dizzy that sometimes she would pass out. It was as though being in the world—or being, itself—had become painful for her. It seemed like a life sentence to absence.

Years later, when I began to love English poetry of the sixteenth and seventeenth centuries, I thought of that sad time. I mean not just John Donne writing explicitly about his illness, "Therefore that He may raise, the Lord throws down." I felt the personal connection even more in his poem "Twickenham Garden," where he exclaims about himself in the garden, "O, self-traitor, I do bring / The spider love, which transubstantiates all, / And can convert Manna to Gall."

My mother's love for us her children and for her husband had brought her, by way of that transubstantiating attic joist, to a galling derangement. The spider love was dismantling her senses. In our overcrowded apartment, negation and absence were presences. In the dark bedroom, isolated as much as possible from sound and light, she declared that only her obligation to her children prevented her from killing herself.

I think of that dark bedroom where she lay every time I read Fulke Greville's poem beginning "Down in the depth of my iniquity." The poem describes how Jesus Christ's presence harrows Hell itself, or harrows the internal Hell of the poet's tormented soul: "Scourging all the spirits infernal /

And uncreated hell with unprivation." Uncreated, unprivation! I thrilled to those redoubled negatives even before I
learned the peculiar, violent theology behind them.

Evil, in the Thomist or Augustinian tradition of the poetry
I was discovering, is an absence, a lack, a privation. As cold
is an absence of heat energy and darkness is an absence of
light energy, the sin is a vacuum in the soul, a painful absence
of Being. In another word of negation Greville uses in that
same poem, the sin is not an entity but rather a "deformity":
the opposite of forming, an un-making. In Donne's phrase,
one becomes a self-traitor. The desperate soul tears a hole in
itself, reduces its own existence.

But why? In a saying of the Talmud, the evil that others do
to us is as nothing compared to the evil we do to ourselves.
Not true for victims of torture, genocide, child abuse, rape,
famine. But true for John Donne and for Dante Alighieri and
for me and many people. Why? How is it that we choose to sin
and wither? That mystery of self-destruction is at the center
of Dante's *Inferno*—perché nostra colpa se ne scipa? Why do
we let our sins destroy us? Despair. The most destructive sin,
worst of sins in that it disables grace, despair is the ultimate
privation, the non-being or unmaking that invades the soul.
Despair is Dante's own sin—accidie, or in the English term
"wanhope." Donne means wanhope when he says, "I have a
sin of fear." The sin hurts, and so does the harrowing presence that floods the hollow of despair with Being.

For years, I tried to understand how much of my mother's
suffering had been "real" and how much was "unreal." How
much came from the concussion's bodily damage to her brain,
and how much was in her mind?

In 1964 the astronaut John Glenn, about to run for a seat
in the United States Senate, slipped and hit his head on a
hotel bathtub. The vertigo, headaches and other symptoms
forced Glenn, the first American to orbit the earth, and a war

hero as well, to abandon his Senate campaign. His symptoms persisted for more than a year before they dwindled enough for him to run again. He was elected to the Senate in 1974. I followed John Glenn's illness through its phases, reading the newspaper stories with a personal interest. For a time, the course of his injury and recovery tipped my thinking about my mother's woe toward the physical, away from the psychological.

Gradually, in the course of a million reconsiderations, that question—body or mind?—came to feel pointless. No one could ever say how much Sylvia Pinsky was depressed by her physical illness, with its cruel limitations, or how much the effects of the joist's glancing blow to her brain were exaggerated by her depression. Beyond those unknowns, there were social realities. Sylvia Pinsky was an intelligent woman, ambitious by nature, but born in 1917 (before passage of the Nineteenth Amendment) into an immigrant family without money. She had much to be depressed about.

As a way to overcome his own spiritual viltade, or cowardice, as his guide Virgil calls it, Dante in the journey down through Hell witnesses, in a descending pageant, the range of ways we can harm ourselves. *Inferno* is the greatest work I know about despair, or as we call it in our contemporary jargon, depression. Fear impels a journey through the terrain of failure and self-destruction. My mother in her sadness and fearfulness shared the same woe—or, as Dante and Donne and Greville called it, the same sin—as those great poets.

None of these thoughts were in my mind when I began trying to make an English version of *Inferno*. As with many things, my *Inferno of Dante* began with random turns of fate from outside combining with quirks, knacks and habits on the inside. The poet and publisher Daniel Halpern was editing an *Inferno* with each canto translated by an American poet. My assignment was Canto XXVIII, where the schismatic Bertran de Born walks along carrying his head, which speaks to Dante—a sight so incredible, says Dante, that he feels afraid to tell it. But since he really saw it, he must.

I enjoyed working on XXVIII, in particular trying to convey the speed of the Italian, as it springs from the syncopated rhyming of terza rima, a form Dante invented for his poem. The technical challenge gave me a pleasure like what can come from an excellent puzzle or a difficult piece of music. The poet assigned to Canto XX decided to abandon it, so I did that one too, about soothsayers and fortune-tellers. Their souls in hell walk with their heads on backward, "Contorted so the eyes' tears fell to wet / The buttocks at their cleft. Truly I wept."

A lifelong mania drives me to think about the vowels and consonants of "fell," "contorted," "tears," "wet," "cleft," "truly" and "wept." I used to play tennis with a clockmaker who had a specialty shop in downtown Wellesley. His minuscule vises and tiny lathes were precise beyond imagining. In a conversation between sets he told me about the hypnotic thrill he felt at calibrating gears triggered by a counterbalancing steel-alloy spring as fine as a hair, all invisible within a polished case. He described looking up from his work to notice that the windows had grown dark. In his occupational trance the clockmaker lost track of time—the same experience I had trying to create idiomatic sentence-melodies in English verses, respectful of Dante's meaning. The springs and escapements of terza rima became hypnotic.

Having finished XX, the canto someone had abandoned, I started to work on Canto I almost covertly, as if it were a video game. I finished it and started toying, with guilty pleasure, with Canto II. I had entered a difficulty I loved. This would be my fourth Canto out of thirty-four. That was nearly an eighth of the entire journey through Hell, I told myself. It was time to confer with Seamus Heaney.

Luckily for me, Seamus was nearby. In the living room of his Cambridge sublet, with kids coming and going, we spent a few hours looking at the Dante versions I had, comparing them with his I and II for the Halpern book. We also talked about his wonderful poems based on the *Inferno*, "Ugolino" and "An Afterwards"—still recent work, then. Toward the end of the day's session he said to me about the *Inferno*, "Do it." And after a pause, with increased emphasis, "Do it quickly." I keep on my desk the medal—somebody's prize for "Excellence in Italian," with a profile of Dante—that Seamus bought for me in a Cambridge junk store.

Many years before I thought about a version of *Inferno*, the Thomistic idea of Hell as an absence, and evil as a privation, was at the heart of *An Explanation of America* (1979). In that book's central section, "Its Great Emptiness," I try to consider the possibility of an American fascism based on xenophobia, brewed in the inherited demons and vacancies of a settler culture, and boiling over viciously amid the sheer overwhelming size of our wide-open spaces.

At the American Embassy in Dublin, as I began a reading from that book, an official interrupted me to announce that we must all leave the building. President Ronald Reagan had been shot. So with Seamus, who had just introduced my reading, and some other Irish poets, I retreated to a pub. After some political discussion, in a tradition shared by Ireland and New Jersey, jokes were told. Seamus told the one about German Hell and Italian Hell. I remember making fun of his attempt at accents—his Germans and Italians all sounded kind of Japanese.

As to *Inferno*, why translate a work that had already been translated into English many times? And why would a Jew translate a Christian epic, or feel qualified to do that? In what way is the hell of wanhope American—let alone Jewish? My answer to those questions is partly a matter of (for lack of a better word) form—a making that is the opposite of despair. Form, like Fulke Greville's "saving God," scourges "uncreated hell with unprivation."

The Italian line Dante used for his *Commedia* contains eleven syllables. The English pentameter line—the many-purposed line of Shakespeare's plays, of John Keats's "Ode to a Nightingale," Wallace Stevens's "Sunday Morning" and Elizabeth Bishop's "One Art"—also averages out to eleven syllables in each line.

Italian words are mostly longer than English words. "Selva oscura" uses more syllables than "dark woods." "Via diritta" uses more syllables than "right road." "Era smarrita" uses more syllables than "was lost." Therefore, if you translate an eleven-syllable line of Italian into an eleven-syllable line of English, you must add padding: some verbal equivalent, however skillfully concealed, of Styrofoam or bubble wrap.

That explains why the translations of Dante I had read seemed slow, compared to the speed and quickness of the Italian terza rima, as it moves deftly among curses, descriptions, insults, praises, flights of imagination, science and song, theology and dialogue. Even the gorgeous and learned blank-verse *Commedia* of Longfellow, who was a professor of Romance languages, uses the line-for-line method. Translating each line of Dante's poem into English, and contriving English sentences to hold the lines together, inevitably leads to padding.

I did it the opposite way: sentences before lines. Following a musical instinct, without thinking about it, I at once began to translate Dante's sentences, contriving English lines that might sound good. My working principle was, in order to get a rhyme, always contract, never expand, while being faithful to that chimera "the literal."

If nothing else, what I did moves along, using far fewer words than any other translation I know, in verse or prose. In the published book, the Italian on the left uses only indentations to mark the terzine, with no vertical space between them; the English on the right has white space between the three-line stanzas: a continuous vertical block on the left, separate three-line units on the right. Otherwise, the en-face format would not work. The English would have leapt ahead by many pages.

Some things are sacrificed. My version fails to put the same words or phrases at the end of a line as in the original. As an example, here are the famous first three lines of *Inferno*:

> *Nel mezzo del cammin di nostra vita*
> *mi retrovai per una selva oscura*
> *che la diritta via era smarrita.*

My English version uses a little under two lines:

> Midway in our life's journey I found myself
> In dark woods, the right road lost.

The poet David Rivard wrote about those lines that "right road lost" has an American quality. Those three syllables, he said, would not be out of place in a blues lyric by Robert Johnson. That observation pleased me by noting the simultaneous values of music, idiom and plainness.

I thought obsessively about the difficulties of syntax, rhymes, enjambment, sentence-tune: all the innumerable counterparts of the watchmaker's gears and levers. On some other, belowground level, I must have been driven by ideas: Dante's depression and my mother's and my own; Dante's improvised, omnivorous relation to cultures and ideas; the relation of Jews like me to Christian realities like the *Commedia* and two deeply Christianized languages, English and Italian. In a more conscious way I was thinking about the terrific monotype illustrations Michael Mazur was working on for the book, and my discussions about the *Commedia* with Michael, whose Italian was much better than mine.

That opening passage describes Dante's experience of despair and his determination to make something good out of it:

> Midway on our life's journey, I found myself
> In dark woods, the right road lost. To tell
> About those woods is hard—so tangled and rough
>
> And savage that thinking of it now, I feel
> The old fear stirring: death is hardly more bitter.
> And yet, to treat the good I found there as well
>
> I'll tell what I saw, though how I came to enter
> I cannot well say, being so full of sleep
> Whatever moment it was I began to blunder
>
> Off the true path. But when I came to stop
> Below a hill that marked one end of the valley
> That had pierced my heart with terror, I looked up
>
> Toward the crest and saw its shoulders already
> Mantled in rays of that bright planet that shows
> The road to everyone, whatever our journey.

Of course, I noted the "old fear" and "that pierced my heart with terror" in that tangled, savage place: the disabling fall into despair. Wanhope. But mainly, I was thinking about sentences as they intersected with lines, the sounds, all the gears and levers that can animate a poem.

In a similar way, when the rest of my family was inspecting a model house we couldn't afford, with the parents trying to solve the problems of five people in a cramped apartment on a dicey street, I must have been thinking, at some level, about those quarrels, wants and tensions. But I was at the piano, trying inexpertly to figure out harmonies and structures and how keys, chords and scales might be related. It wasn't my destined art, but that musical tinkering kept the surface of my mind busy and purposeful, whatever might have been churning further down.

The difficult mother can become a cliché. I am trying to tell about something more immediate and individual than any stereotype—and more abnormal. For example, a bit more than two years after the concussion, my mother set out to attend my bar mitzvah ceremony in October of 1953, but she missed it—who knows why? She was there in the Orthodox shul on Second Avenue, but when the moment came for me to sing the haftorah portion, she was gone. To make the point even more clear (or dark?), ten years later she missed my brother Richard's bar mitzvah entirely. When Richard sang his haftorah, Ellen Pinsky also missed his performance because she was at her mother-in-law's house, trying to persuade the bar mitzvah boy's mother to attend the ceremony. Something had gone wrong about a hat, as ten years before something went wrong about the refreshments. My mother also refused to attend her mother's funeral.

I include the information about her heavy absence at those ceremonies—a powerful non-being—in my "Poem with Refrains." The refrains come from sixteenth century poems, including one by Fulke Greville: "Absence my presence is, strangeness my grace; / With them that walk against me is my sun." That poem also pays tribute to Sylvia Pinsky's anarchic wisecracks. It describes her in old age, watching television:

> She sees the minister of the Nation of Islam
> On television, though she's half-blind in one eye.

His bow tie is lime, his jacket crocodile green.
Vigorously he denounces the Jews who traded in slaves,
The Jews who run the newspapers and the banks.
"I see what this guy is mad about now," she says,
"It must have been some Jew that sold him the suit."

Like her joke about Hitler, holding a bit of her hair on her husband's upper lip, this remark has a reckless quality I admire. The poem was reprinted in the *Newark Star-Ledger*. The Newark poet Amiri Baraka responded to it positively, saying that he had been waiting for some Jewish poet to write from experience, with understanding, about Jews and Black people in American cities. "At last, a Jew who gets it," or something like that.

Sylvia Pinsky, truly remarkable in her gifts as well as her miseries, had won, from an unlikely source, a bit of recognition she deserved.

XVIII

All of the Above

M Y MINI-STROKE came on April Fool's Day, 2020, not long after I began writing this book. Sitting with my laptop in a room just off the front hall, I saw Ellen walking toward our mail, which had just thudded through the door slot.

Looking up, I had in mind some little joke about the Covid-19 pandemic and our mail. I intended to say something like, We don't need to soak the catalogues in bleach solution before we toss them into the recycle bin. But what came out of my mouth was more like "local gallant logs," "each notion," "chinblains," and "bicycle sniff." As in poetry, rearranged consonants.

When you play with clay or paint or a musical instrument, the physical material can psychoanalyze you. It shows you what you have been thinking and feeling. The same with the physical sounds of speech. Alienated by a mishap in the brain, the stuff of meaning can plunge beyond the subconscious, into a bramble of confusion. My words with their transposed consonants resembled a writing exercise. But a cerebral zit had turned that possible lesson in levels of meaning, or in chance and intuition, into the possible Hell of self-exile.

There was no delusion. I knew clearly that what I was saying didn't make enough sense, but each try came out as babble. Ellen, accustomed to verbal clowning of a certain kind, wanted me to stop it. At first my inability seemed funny to both of us. Looking a little alarmed, she smiled, and said to me:

"Could you possibly stop fucking around for one minute?"

The episode lasted five or ten minutes, terrifying for both of us. So far, the temporary symptoms have not returned. The medical term is "TIA," a "transient ischemic attack." The comforting "transient" seems to apply—no lasting effects.

Or is there a lasting effect in my feeling there was something in character about the event, reflecting my destiny, or my ways of being? Could that deforming yet comical attack have made my writing slightly worse? Or better? *Yes, both*, the Fool in me declares.

The brief April Fool's Day attack of tangled consonants remains an example for me of dread and laughter in a single chord. I thought of my mother's concussion and its sad, prolonged (far from "transient") aftermath. In a less rational association, in the days after the TIA my mind lurched back to September 11, 2001. Maybe it was the word "attack."

On September 10, 2001, I boarded the early-morning American Airlines plane from Boston: Flight 11, landing in L.A. before lunchtime. By one o'clock I was in a studio with the masterful voice actors Dan Castanaletta, Nancy Cartwright and Yeardley Smith, rehearsing and recording an episode of *The Simpsons*. In the episode, "Little Girl in the Big Ten," Lisa Simpson, posing as a college student, attends a campus poetry reading given by a self-important, hammy poet named "Robert Pinsky," played by me as voice actor.

Among friends, I am sometimes considered funny. In

that recording studio, it was like trying to play hoops with NBA players. The way star characters in a movie care for a secondary character who has trouble climbing through the burning skyscraper, the actors helped me. They suggested line readings, like an understated voicing of "ka-ching." In the script, Lisa Simpson is thrilled that I will be reading my poem "Impossible to Tell." I recorded some lines from the poem and finished my scenes with the actors in time for a quick supper with family in L.A. By eight-thirty Pacific time I was ready for sleep.

The next morning, preparing for the flight back to Boston, I turned on the hotel room TV to see stories about a plane crash minutes ago in New York. One of the morning-show hosts was nattering about the "accident." I remember thinking how stupid he was. The plane had hit a Manhattan tower—clearly that was no accident. I turned off the TV and went downstairs for a car to the airport.

A few minutes after we left the hotel, the car radio said another airplane had hit the Pentagon. That information made me reconsider my ant-like behavior of heading to LAX as planned. I was being nearly as stupid as that morning-show personality. I asked the driver to please turn around and take me back to the hotel.

If anyone asks me about my experience of 9/11, I have to decide whether to tell about *The Simpsons*. And the reverse is true. When asked what it was like to be on *The Simpsons*, should I explain that it was my experience of 9/11? That I was on that same American Flight 11, one day before? Dread and laughter. The fusion of a historic disaster and an animated sitcom, mass deaths and comedy, came to seem almost personal, or even characteristic.

Arguably, that feeling—taking it personally—is grandiose: consistent with the self-centered, yellow-headed version of myself that I play in the episode. In a conversation over pizza after the poetry reading, my character starts boasting to the college students about his doings in the White House. The words "White House" remind Lisa that she has to finish her school project due the next day, her model of the White House made of popsicle sticks. She bolts for home, and as she leaves, my line is, "Did she put in for the pizza?"

"Impossible to Tell," the poem that "I" perform in the *Simpsons* episode, is a work of grief. An elegy for my dead friend Elliot Gilbert, the poem contains full-scale jokes. Mel Brooks is cited, along with Bashō, in another example of hopping between mourning and comedy, with jagged discontinuities and buried connections.

On September 12, the people who ran *The Simpsons* invited me to a table-read of a new script, an event they decided not to cancel. The actors and writers arrived to the rehearsal space quietly, saying very little. The head producer did not make any speeches or disclaimers or references to the tragedy. No pieties or bromides, maybe something like a sober, "Let's get to work."

The voice actors, seated with the rest of us around a big conference table, sight-read from their scripts with skillful intensity. Their timing and subtle teamwork again reminded me of the NBA. The new script was funny. We laughed a lot. Then, as soon as the session ended, we all rose from the table. With no transition, the held-back mood of our arrival came back. In the same stricken quiet as the rest of the country, everybody murmured brief goodbyes and left.

For five days, I remained in the hotel as a guest of the Fox network, with all air travel in the United States indefinitely suspended. Each day brought a new reservation for a flight home to Boston, and each day the flight was canceled. Thanks to the *Simpsons* production team, I was cared for. They took me to dinner, and I heard stories about, for example, what they felt as Fox's lack of support for a show that bewildered the people who ran the network. At the Emmy Awards ceremony when *The Simpsons* won its prizes, Fox didn't send anybody to represent the network.

Cheap-to-make "reality" shows, the form that would elevate Donald Trump, were having their first wave of success. Two of *The Simpsons*' cast invented a new Fox reality show. It would consist entirely of people kicking one another in the groin. "Owwww" and "Eeeegh" and maybe "Oh! My balls!" would be the show's only dialogue.

In those post-9/11 days of grief and anxiety, calls for poetry emerged from many directions. As when people are confronted with funerals and weddings, but on a larger scale, 9/11 created a thirst for poetry—whatever the word meant. Eloquence and ceremony were in demand. Individuals and institutions, print media and broadcast media, wanted recommendations of specific poems. I had said that "Consultant in Poetry to the Library of Congress" was more noble and more democratic than the Royalist brand "Laureate." Now I was being consulted, about a large matter. Put up or shut up.

I combed the internet and my memory for poems that might answer the need. In the L.A. hotel room provided by Fox, between visits with grandson Sam and his parents in Venice, or evenings with my new *Simpsons* friends, I read and I thought.

I never did get on a plane from L.A. home to Boston. By the time airlines were operating again, I flew from L.A. to Cleveland for a September 16 speaking engagement at the splendid old Main Library building of the Cleveland Public Library. From the library's high vestibule ceiling hung the famous Terrestrial Globe. On display near the entry was a portrait of Langston Hughes, editor of his senior-class yearbook at Cleveland's Central High School. The setting and the occasion made me anxious in a different way from the mere stage fright at the *Simpsons* taping five days before. Again, in order to perform at all I needed to hide the anxiety—my life-long habit. But this was a different kind of pressure, with the possibility of failure on a different scale.

I talked to the audience about scale: the massive size and complexity of the airplanes and the buildings they crashed into, the immense, engineered forces and materials in the target buildings and also in the weaponized airplanes. The magnitude of everything involved included the mass media that conveyed the event, immediately, to so many millions of us. I reached for a contrast between that "enormity"—in both senses of the word, outrageous horror as well as massive quantities—and poetry, with its inherently human scale, embodied in the quality of a voice.

I tried to focus on each individual reader saying a poem's words aloud, or imagining how saying them aloud would feel, while voicing the words internally. Intimate, human scale can have the power to penetrate the way fine oil penetrates rock. I gave that notion to the audience, knowing that some of them would embrace what I said, some would reject or ignore it. Different people would understand it or misunderstand it, remember it or forget it, doze off or feel engaged.

And I read to them. About reading poetry to an audience, Leonard Cohen says when you read aloud the word "butterfly" you should not take it as your opportunity to fly about and befriend flowers, or to imply that you love butterflies more than other people do. In that spirit, I read aloud four poems I had settled on in the L.A. hotel room, by Marianne Moore, Edwin Arlington Robinson, Czesław Miłosz, and Carlos Drummond de Andrade.

My memory of nervously, earnestly relying on those poems in the Main Library's noble, communal space—"Public" in the institution's very name—on September 16, 2001, collides in my mind with the September 10 experience the week before of trying to keep up with the actors Dan Castanaletta and Nancy Cartwright. The two settings can stand for the still-evolving place of poetry in American culture: making it up as we go along.

Miłosz's "Incantation," with its almost pedagogical tone, is in a way radically unlike American poetry. The very first words are, "Human reason is beautiful and invincible"— words so unlikely for an American poet to write that some readers assume Miłosz is merely joking. I don't think so. Human reason, the poem declares, "Opens the congealed fist of the past." The concluding lines link science ("Philo-Sophia") with poetry:

> Beautiful and very young are Philo-Sophia
> And poetry, her ally in the service of the good.
> As late as yesterday Nature celebrated their birth,
> The news was brought to the mountains by a unicorn
>   and an echo.
> Their friendship will be glorious, their time has no
>   limit.
> Their enemies have delivered themselves to
>   destruction.

Less oratorical, Edwin Arlington Robinson's "The House on the Hill" ends with almost monotone lines that in a different way from "Incantation" felt right to read aloud a few days after 9/11:

> There is ruin and decay
> In the House on the Hill:
> They are all gone away,
> There is nothing more to say.

"There is nothing more to say." That is Robinson's extreme, flat response to his poem's earlier question about the abandoned house: "Why is it then we stray / Around that shrunken sill?" That "Why?" is a pained vocal shrug I can imagine in the voice of Elizabeth Bishop or James Joyce or, in fact, Sylvia Pinsky. The voice says to itself, "What did you expect?"

Robinson's understatement makes an interesting counterpoint with Marianne Moore's more ebullient "What Are Years?" with its image of the soul in defeat acceding to mortality, but triumphantly. The soul in its imprisonment rises, Moore writes, as "the sea in a chasm, struggling to be / free and unable to be, / in its surrendering / finds its continuing." Moore's rhymes and rhyme-like echoes have the quality of doom-ridden laughter. The captive bird, she says, grows taller as he sings and "steels / his form straight up" to perform his "mighty singing." The nervy adjective "mighty" for the canary has an intricate courage and humor. Even the title, "What Are Years?" has a comic undertone, to my ear. One answer to that title question might be that years are what will obliterate everybody and everything. But I also hear a prideful, smiling dismissal: "What are years to me?—I'm busy trying to make my poem."

Drummond de Andrade's "Souvenir of the Ancient World," in Mark Strand's translation, gathers its wave of feeling from a quotidian expedition to a public garden where Clara, whoever she may be, brings "the children." Everything is quiet. Bicycles pass. And in the final lines:

> The children looked at the sky: it was not forbidden.
> Mouth, nose, eyes were open. There was no danger.
> What Clara feared were the flu, the heat, the insects.
> Clara feared missing the eleven o'clock trolley:
> She waited for letters slow to arrive,
> She couldn't always wear a new dress. But she strolled
>   in the garden, in the morning!
> They had gardens, they had mornings in those days!

No subject is more grave than the loss of innocence on a global, historical scale. The poem's last line is the grave, lyrical equivalent of a punch line.

In Louis Malle's movie *Atlantic City*, Burt Lancaster, playing an elderly small-time New Jersey gangster, says to a younger man: "The Atlantic Ocean was something then. You should have seen the Atlantic Ocean in those days."

What are years, what is the wounded Atlantic Ocean these days, what is there to say about the abandoned house, what are the poetry-bro guys of the *Simpsons* episode supposed to be thinking, with words from "Impossible to Tell" painted on their bare chests, what are we to make of the hijacked flights, the religious fanatics and all those deaths, including the passengers who somehow brought the hijacked Flight 93 down to crash in rural Pennsylvania, instead of the Capitol in Washington? What is laughter, what are tears? The poetry answer, or the poetry way of putting the question, is like my joke of a battle cry or heraldic motto: All of the Above.

A decade after *Sadness And Happiness* with its jittering, headlong jumps from woodmanship to baseball hits and errors to Central Square, in *History of My Heart* I try to include laughter and music, desire and catastrophe, in a less frantic kind of movement. The manic inclusiveness, the why-not drive toward "all of the above" persists. But the later title poem "History of My Heart" is more explicit and linear, candid about my mother's brain injury and (maybe) less like my own transient ischemic attack years later:

>   . . . Shrill flutes,
> Oboes and cymbals of doom. My poor mother fell,
>
> And after the accident loud noises and bright lights
> Hurt her. And heights. She went down stairs
>   backwards,
> Sometimes with one arm on my small brother's
>   shoulder.

Over the years, she got better. But I was lost in music;
The cold brazen bow of the saxophone, its weight
At thumb, neck and lip, came to a bloodwarm life

Like ltalo's flashlight in the hand. In a white
Jacket and pants with a satin stripe I aspired
To the roughneck elegance of my Grandfather Dave.

Sometimes, playing in a bar or at a high school dance,
I felt my heart following after a capacious form,
Sexual and abstract, in the thunk, thrum,

Thrum, come-wallow and then a little screen
Of quicker notes goosing to a fifth higher, winging
To clang-whomp of a major seventh: listen to *me*

Listen to *me*, the heart says in reprise until sometimes
In the course of giving itself it flows out of itself
All the way across the air, in a music piercing

As the kids at the beach calling from the water *Look,*
Look at me, to their mothers, but out of itself, into
The listener the way feeling pretty or full of erotic reverie

Makes the one who feels seem beautiful to the
    beholder
Witnessing the idea of the giving of desire—nothing
    more wanted
Than the little singing notes of wanting—the heart

Yearning further into giving itself into the air, breath
Strained into song emptying the golden bell it comes
    from,
    The pure source poured altogether out and away.

XIX

"He Does Not Come to Coo"

I N 2005, I went to North Korea. The occasion was a World
Festival of Peace based in Seoul, sponsored by the Manhae Foundation, to celebrate the seventy-fifth anniversary
of Korea's independence from the imperial power of Japan.
The logo of the festival, posted everywhere, was an image
based on the Reunification Flag used at the Olympic Games.
It shows the two countries reunited as one Korea.

The festival brought to Seoul poets from around the world.
Each of us had been asked to write a poem about our theme:
peace. There were panels, readings and lectures. I was asked
to give a talk on the subject of "Peace and Poetry."

I also got arrested. Or, not to exaggerate, I was briefly
sequestered and detained by the authorities, while crossing
the border from the Republic of Korea into the Democratic
People's Republic of Korea. More important, I learned a little
about the Korean national hero and poet Manhae, the pen
name of Han Yong-un (1879–1944).

Manhae was also a scholar, a reformist Buddhist monk,
a politician and the principal author of the Korean Declaration of Independence. He has been described as combining

achievements of Thomas Jefferson, Walt Whitman, and Harriet Tubman—all of that attained by someone born in 1879, the same year as the less-many-sided American businessman poet Wallace Stevens.

Scholars have said that his knowledge of Chinese as well as Japanese poetry enabled his sophisticated mastery of plain language. There may be many English-language equivalents of that literary distinction, from Ben Jonson to Frank O'Hara, but I can't think of a comparison for his transformation of Korean Buddhism into something more democratic than older traditions. Among other things, Manhae got rid of celibacy as a general doctrine for monks and in his own life. His poems make one idiomatic gesture of the erotic, the political and the spiritual. Thanks to Francine Cho's commanding, persuasively refined English translations, I began reading Manhae's poems in the volume *Everything Yearned For*. The unadorned poems of yearning attain a mystical blend of sexual love and love of country.

On a less lofty note, during that trip sponsored by the Manhae Foundation I received an email from my wise-guy children. I read it on the flight from San Francisco to Seoul. One of them had discovered somewhere a list of actual titles North Korean television had given to the dynastic leader Kim Jong-il, including: "World's Greatest Writer," "Master of the Computer Who Surprised the World," "Eternal Bosom of Hot Love" and "Supreme Commander at the Forefront of the Struggle Against Imperialism and the United States."

The email chain among my children, which they forwarded to me, turned out to be prophetic. In her message attaching that list of preposterous titles, Elizabeth wrote to Nicole: "Not at all sure it's okay to send this to Dad at this moment, but I can't help but think it's apropos. Also, his incarceration would make a real good story."

Elizabeth's words came into my mind on the long bus ride

we poets of many nations took from Seoul to the remote, beautiful Kumgang Mountains of North Korea. Some of the Korean poets in our bus were in tears as we got near the border. For those born there, the North called up deep family connections and memories. For all of the Koreans, the emotional charge of entering the North was something I and the poets from France, Russia, Turkey, Brazil, Nigeria, and India could only try to imagine.

The common language our group used on that bus ride was Spanish. In that language, with our varying competence, we discussed our trip and the expectation of giving a joint reading with North Korean poets. They were scheduled to join us in the evening, after the Peace Ceremony at the Manhae Maeul, Baekdamsa Temple high on the mountain. In English, our Korean hosts explained again the severe restrictions imposed by the Democratic People's Republic. No cell phones, no film cameras, all printed matter severely limited to our own poetry, to be inspected. As we approached the frontier, we noticed a series of solitary armed soldiers posted along the road, at attention, a hundred yards apart. Tuğrul Tanyol, Jean-Michel Maulpoix, Marina Colasanti, Mani Rao and I remarked on los soldados isolados, separados uno a uno.

At the frontier, the people in charge of our bus requested that "Pinsky-san"—the oldest poet on the bus—exit first, walking from the bus to where the border turnstile was manned by two tall soldiers, in spotless uniforms much swankier than those worn by the lonely-looking soldados we had just seen stationed along the highway. I approached the gateway carrying my overnight bag, my passport, and the Korean documents we had been given, with a Korean photo ID hanging from a ribbon around my neck. The high boots and stylish caps of those border guards recalled images from World War II movies about Nazis. Both of the tall, unsmiling young border guards were handsome in a swaggering way that suited their tailored uniforms.

The one at the gateway booth took my American passport between two fingers and scowled at it. He glanced at
my Korean papers, and with no eye contact he gestured me
into a glass-walled cubicle. From there, I watched my fellow poets pass one by one through the checkpoint to a lobby
on the other side. After a while, two other poets from our
party were sent to join me, the three of us crowded into that
little glass room. The situation remained funny, but a bit
nervous-making. The three of us, with no idea why we had
been separated out, watched the others file out of the lobby
to board a different, North Korean bus on the other side. It
seemed like the joke of my daughters' email exchange was
becoming a reality.

We detainees bantered together, with a dash of anxiety, in
a mix of Spanish and English. Finally, we too were ushered
onto the new bus to join our companions headed for the celebration of peace and poetry. After we were seated, there was
more waiting while our South Korean guides had a long talk
with the elegantly scary border guards. After half an hour of
intense discussion in Korean, our guides came back on board,
our bus drove on, and we arrived at the regime's version of a
Western luxury hotel, high in a mountain pass.

On the ride there, as we poets questioned our South
Korean hosts about what had happened at the border, somebody came up with the useful Spanish word "cohecho,"
which has a literal meaning something like "get-it-done" or
"fertilizer." A cohecho is drink money, a lubricant. Those tall
sentries in jackboots had requested a bribe. A few hundred
dollars, I think. My misdemeanor, beyond being an American, was that my passport photo was full-face while the
Korean ID photo dangling from a lanyard on my neck was
three-quarters. One of the other poets had not removed the
film from her camera. The whole thing was what some people
might call a New Jersey transaction, raised (or lowered) to the
level of a totalitarian state.

High in the Kumgang mountain landscape, surrounded by natural beauty, were a Buddhist temple and our hotel. On a fifty-foot billboard in front of the hotel was a mural depicting Kim Jong-il, "Greatest Saint Who Rules with Extensive Magnanimity" in the list my daughters sent me. The Most Beloved Insightful Leader was depicted sitting on a bench, surrounded by flowers and an adoring cluster of small children. In the hotel itself, everything—the lobby furniture, the light fixtures, the bed, the fish soup breakfast—seemed to be made by people who had heard descriptions of such things, with no actual experience of them. (That shallow, touristic impression felt all the more problematic, remembered years later, after Donald Trump's declaration that he "fell in love with" the Heaven-Sent Hero's son and successor.)

At dinner that evening, we waited for our North Korean counterparts. Over dessert, it was announced that they had been delayed by another engagement, and regretted they would not be able to join us as planned. Their no-show reminded me that in my talk to the conference I had decided to make my theme negatives and absences.

I quoted Gerard Manley Hopkins's poem on the idea of peace, with its meditation of Christ as a dove, the traditional bird of peace. The poem's word "brood" applies to the bird hatching its young but also entails "brooding" in the sense of a strained, dark meditation. Hopkins expresses impatience, even anger, with any sugary idea of Christ as the Prince of Peace. "When Peace here does house" his poem says, "He comes with work to do, he does not come to coo, / He comes to brood and sit." I liked the negative, even comical pugnacious daring of "he does not come to coo."

That phrase might suggest something we poets shared, coming though we did from our different countries on every continent, each culture with its various roles for our ancient art, changing and persisting in the still young and sometimes terrifying twenty-first century: not to coo. The absence of our North Korean counterparts that evening was a small example of large concerns, within our art and beyond it.

"He does not come to coo" strikes a disruptive note like Emily Dickinson's poem portraying the harbor of Peace as a delusion, but then reasserting its promise in a pleasingly negative, grudging way:

> I many times thought Peace had come
> When Peace was far away—
> As Wrecked Men—deem they sight the Land—
> At Centre of the Sea—
>
> And struggle slacker—but to prove
> As hopelessly as I—
> How many the fictitious Shores—
> Before the Harbor be—

"How many the fictitious Shores": the infinite, manifold possibilities and impossibilities of imagination, its hopes and illusions. Dickinson's contrary way of evoking the Shores of Peace and its Harbor led me back to Manhae. His poems that merge spiritual love, romantic love and patriotic love also embrace opposites, including life and death. In Francisca Cho's translation, Manhae's poem "Come" begins with images of peace:

> Should anyone chase you, hide in the blossoms.
> I'll turn into a butterfly and light upon the ones you
>   hide among.
> Then your pursuer won't find you.
> Come, please come. It's time.
>
> Come in to my arms, my breast is soft there.

> Though I'm soft as water, I'm a golden sword and an
> iron shield to protect you.

The refrain, "Come, please come. It's time," takes on a different feeling in the poem's conclusion:

> Come in to my death, my death is always ready for you.
> Should anyone chase you, stand behind my death.
> In death, emptiness and omnipotence are one.
> Love's death is at once infinite, everlasting.
> In death, battleship and fortress become dust.
> In death, the strong and the weak are companions.
> Then your pursuer won't catch you.
> Come, please come. It's time.

The word "death," seven times in six lines! Mortality here includes comfort and urgency, together. The roots of Manhae's poetry can be read as erotic or nationalistic, psychological or political, personal or communal. The multiple levels might represent not a taste for allegory, and not a delight in a poetry of hidden meanings—but rather, art's quality of inclusion: not to convey that a love affair is a secret code for patriotism, but to understand how the human soul enacts both, with the principle of urgency in the shadow of death.

Negatives, sometimes double or triple, appear in many of Manhae's poems. "I haven't seen your heart," says the refrain of "Your Heart." "Don't," says the refrain of "First Kiss." "It's not for nothing that I love you," says "Love's Reasons." Even a poem of devotion has the refrain "Don't Doubt": "If you doubt me, then your error of doubt / and my fault of sorrow will cancel each other." And in "Don't Go": "That's not the light of compassion from Buddha's brow; it's the flash from a demon's eyes." The refrain of that poem is, "Turn around—don't go to that place. I hate it."

The negative! It cheered me up to find it in the work of Korea's national poet. In a certain way, the negative is near the heart of poetry itself: a negation that by implication says to politics, *No, you are not all there is, there is also the human body*; and to the human body, poetry implicitly dissents, *No, you are not all there is, there is also spiritual yearning*; and to spiritual yearning, poetry says, *No, you are not all there is, there is also sexual pleasure*; and to sexual pleasure, *No, you are not all there is, there is also politics.*

The art says no to all, and includes all. Unruly, it welcomes conflict, paradox and negation. There in Seoul I quoted the Yiddish poet Zische Landau, who said that whatever Yiddish poetry might be, it could not be merely "the Rhyme Department of the Jewish Labor Movement." That is, poetry does not merely put particular feelings and ideas into language, it creates an experience that reminds us of something beyond any particular feelings and ideas. Always "not this"—always beyond, always in process, headed somewhere new and contradictory. In the Soviet days of Eastern Europe, a Polish poet has said, the most ambitious poet was the state: it wanted to control all the metaphors. Manhae's *Everything Yearned For* wants all the metaphors to remain open.

The encounter with Manhae came at a point in my life when I had to reconcile my habitual, defensive mistrust of official recognitions like "Poet Laureate" with the possibly honorable or at least useful potential of such things. Maybe it was time, finally, for me to stop punishing the world for all those Ds in Citizenship it had given me, back in the eighth grade. It might be time for Pinsky-san to get over it.

At Manhae Maeul, on the spectacular winding path up the mountain to the Baekdamsa Temple, there was a ceremonial unveiling of poems on the theme of peace by poets from around the world. Framed copies of the poems, handwritten by each poet, were hung along the path. In the ceremony, honor and embarrassment, silliness and magnitude, stupidity and meaning, conducted their ancient ballet of opposites. Our group dispersed to gaze at the poems, in a scene like an art opening but with the spectacular mountain view all around us.

The poem I wrote for the occasion, "Stupid Meditation on Peace," has for an epigraph the same six syllables by Gerard Manley Hopkins I quoted in my lecture: "He does not come to coo." "Insomniac monkey-mind," I begin, "ponders the Dove, / Symbol not only of Peace but sexual / Love, the couple nestled and brooding."

"Stupid Meditation" proposes that peace could be attained by sending all human males between the ages of fourteen and twenty-five to the moon, "or better yet Mars": a negative way to stress the difficulty of attaining peace—the difficulty, even, of conceiving peace. The word "stupid" in the title may be a way of speaking to myself as a teenage boy who muttered that word like a mantra, so different from a seasoned navigator of loss like Manhae.

> Monkey-mind envies the male Dove
> Who equally with the female secretes
> Pigeon-milk for the young from his throat.
>
> . . . Is peace merely a vacuum, the negative
> Of creation, or the absence of war?
> The teaching says Peace is a positive energy.
>
> Still something in me resists that sweet milk,
> My mind resembles my restless, inferior cousin
> Who fires his shit in handfuls from his cage.

XX

American Signs

I N 1994 I spent some weeks in Jacksonville, Illinois, where the main industry was hog-farming. A foundation had designed a program for rural communities rarely visited by writers. The idea was to visit schools, talk to civic groups, maybe plan public events, returning a year later for a follow-up visit.

A local saying was, Springfield got the Illinois capital, Jacksonville got a prison, the school for the visually impaired, and the school for the deaf. There were also two colleges. Illinois College and MacMurray College. MacMurray had to close a couple of years ago, for financial reasons.

On what had once been Jacksonville's main street, a handsome courthouse remained among defunct neighbors: a long-closed luncheonette, a bar, a dry-goods and clothing store. Storefronts were boarded up by plywood smeared with faded graffiti. For breakfast every morning I drove a rental car from my motel to a chain restaurant a couple of miles down Route 72. In the sad old story, retail had moved to the highway—possibly as a stop on the way to Amazon. Jacksonville was not what it used to be.

People in the town made me feel welcome. Maybe they recognized a fellow provincial. At both colleges I gave talks from a writer's viewpoint on Willa Cather and Carl Sandburg, choices I hoped fit the locale. I also spoke about works by Isaac Babel, Emily Dickinson and Ralph Ellison. My theme was rage and gratitude, in different blends and kinds, between individual characters and their communities—for example, William Faulkner, still so disliked in a personal way, generations later, by many people in Oxford, Mississippi, the hometown he obsessively teased. (Some say that the local family he fictionalizes as the low-life Snopeses consider themselves an old and eminent local clan.)

From Faulkner's *The Hamlet*, with its rural small-town fabric, I read the extended, lyrical description of childlike Ike Snopes courting a cow he loves, sexually. It was fun to contrast that rhapsodic language with the speech of Ike's cousin I. O. Snopes, in his ratty frock coat and his pseudo-scholarly eyeglasses with no lenses:

> Flesh is weak, and it wants but little here below. Because sin's in the eye of the beholder; cast the beam outen your neighbors' eyes and out of sight is out of mind. A man can't have his good name drug in the alleys. The Snopes name has done held its head up too long in this country to have no such reproaches against it like stock-diddling.

The tatters of ruined language, with biblical clichés embedded in the misery and falsehoods of an American backwater. This passage seemed to be as funny and as tragic amid the cornfields of southern Illinois, near the collapsed downtown of Jacksonville, as on the Jersey Shore.

For occasions at the local colleges we invited visitors from Jacksonville and other nearby towns. The students felt themselves to be, in various ways, somewhere between those community guests—who might be their parents or aunts and uncles—and us academic hosts. That was a feeling I recognized: the American college as an island territory, valued but a bit alien, for many of us among the students, the teachers, the community visitors. Our shared efforts in the classroom might be as faulty, in a way, as the eloquence of I. O. Snopes. But like Snopes's imperfect creator, the failed poet Faulkner, we were giving it an ambitious try.

Faulkner, Dickinson, Ellison and other American writers gave us an exhilarating sense of a national enterprise, related to sixteenth century translations of the Bible, to the cursed heritage of slavery, to a million different forms of provincialism and aspiration, nativism and immigration. In Jacksonville, adding the stories of Isaac Babel, with his Jewish gangsters in the seaport of Odessa, provided a different version of the historical nightmare (or dream?) and an imagined, desperately thirsted-for awakening—for Babel, the Revolution he idealized that silenced him and killed him.

Meaningful in a different way from those discussions at the colleges, and profoundly new to me, was visiting the School for the Visually Impaired and the School for the Deaf, along with the prison: what Jacksonville got when Springfield got the capital.

My first day at the School for the Deaf began with a poetry reading by a number of students presenting their work. A few classes were combined for the occasion. Waiting for things to start, the crowd of kids were jabbering to one another in an American Sign equivalent of noisy. I asked the teacher sitting next to me what the sign is for "quiet down." With a smile, she held one finger to her lips. A minute later the school principal stood up and held one finger to her lips. The hall went still immediately, as the principal signed her opening remarks into a perfect silence of both voice and signing.

Several of the adults in the room were graduate students.

These were hearing-able people who came to the school as interns, so they could improve their accents in American Sign. They were trying to pick up the melodic flow that makes any language distinct and rapid: the fluidity that comes from immersion.

The young student poets that day did everything at once. They vocalized as they signed. Many of them also danced and mimed, along with the melody of gesture. The teacher at my side whispered simultaneous translations for me, so I listened as I watched. One of the graduate student interns showed me different signs for "poetry." As I remember, poetry delivered in Sign is indicated by a fountain-like burst of five fingers opening out from the heart. Poetry read from a page is indicated by the sign for reading, but with the two fingers on the text of the other arm dancing rather than walking. For poetry heard phonetically, possibly along with Sign, the two fingers do their page-reading dance as they spring out from the heart.

That event, with the kids exuberantly vocalizing while they signed, expressive from head to toe, added to my sense of Ezra Pound's metaphor of poetry as a centaur: a being of both body and mind. The reading in Sign brought me back to my childhood and trying to echo the shapes of particular sentences with my fingernails on the headboard.

One student poet that first day presented a poem expressing her pain at being excluded from her older sister's wedding ceremony, because of how her voice and pronunciation sounded to people. She had something to give, something she could have added to that family occasion, her poem said— amplifying for me the tremendous verb "said."

Recently, an MFA student at Boston University asked me to approve his plan to take, as one of his requirements outside of Creative Writing, a course in American Sign, rather than the more customary choices in literature, ethnic studies, linguistics, etc. He had no immediate need to learn Sign, but in the way of his generation he told me that his identity had made him feel marginalized. Deaf people, too, are marginalized, he said, and he thought the parallel experience would make this an appropriate course. I agreed. I told him I thought another benefit of studying Sign, for a poet, might be to re-emphasize the bodily nature of poetry, with related kinds of energy circulating among empathy, physicality and language.

My most intense and prolonged work in Jacksonville was at the School for the Visually Impaired, where I regularly attended a poetry class. In the nature of the school's purpose, the number of students a teacher could deal with in any class was small. In our group, there were four students. Some of them fit into both categories, visually impaired as well as deaf. Thanks partly to their gifted teacher, I can still remember each of those teenagers as an individual.

At the first meeting I attended, I heard about an ambitious old-fashioned exercise they had completed, a writing assignment based on the "General Prologue" to Geoffrey Chaucer's *Canterbury Tales*. (To the credit of Illinois, by law every book published in the state must be available in braille.) The students in our group were asked to write a poem based, as in Chaucer's "Prologue," on a person of some specific professional or social type.

One boy had written a particularly successful poem, wowing the other students and the teacher with its vivid details. He was a good-looking, amiable young man, a champion swimmer. With his permission, the teacher showed me his poem that she and the class admired. She warned me that many of the students at her school were often angry. Normal for people their age—speaking of types—and for some of them, adolescent anger was redoubled by the large and small woes of impaired vision.

The boy's well-written poem was in the first person, and

the narrating character's profession was assassin. The details included the sensation felt through the knife's handle of the point penetrating through soft tissue to grate against bone, with blood spurting up around the blade. I had noted that the swimmer seemed able to see better than other students. He would hold a typed page close to his face and read from it quite well. His condition, the poetry teacher explained, was progressive as well as incurable. His vision would be gone entirely within a year or two.

After I got to know the students a little, they told me another example of teenage anger that had erupted during the brief regime of a substitute teacher they didn't like. Their classmate Linda, the youngest in the group, had really lost it, they told me with a lot of hilarity. I can't recall what they said the teacher had done to repel all of them, and Linda in particular. Linda was the smallest person in the group, an imaginative child, soft-spoken but always ready to speak in discussions. On the occasion that amused them all, Linda got so angry she started swinging her cane ferociously at that substitute teacher, so that the others had to physically hold her back. While her classmates told me the story, Linda smiled shyly.

For some of the deaf kids, I was told, anger might be less powerful than a sense of rejection, as with that memorable poem about being excluded from a sister's wedding ceremony. The speech of a deaf person can bewilder or alienate some people in some settings. The hurt from that response accumulates. Children who attend open houses for prospective students at the School for the Deaf, I was told, sometimes gave terrible, immediate evidence of that social pain. The potential student, as part of the visit, would stay overnight in a dormitory and attend a few classes. When the time came to get back into the family car and return home, some of the children would break down weeping. Returning to their previous daily life marked the loss of a new feeling—in that dormitory and those classrooms—of being normal: feeling, to use an ironic phrase, at home. That was another example of the social powers of speech.

I read aloud poems I liked to the students, who had a braille edition of *The Norton Anthology of Poetry*. The teacher provided me with typed-out copies of what they wrote in braille—extra work for her, as she did not say.

After each class session, the teacher and I chatted for a few minutes about what had happened in the day's session and what we might do next time. The afternoon before the last class I would attend until my return the following year, she hesitantly put a suggestion to me. Might I write a poem for the students, about our work together? It would mean a lot to them if I could do that, and present it to them the next day.

I explained that when I write a poem it proceeds a bit like a shopping mall. First the land is acquired. Then it is surveyed. After a time, heavy equipment comes in to prepare the terrain and dig foundations for the buildings . . . and so forth. And at the end, after the construction crews and the decorators and the painters have done their work . . . then comes the final draft: people drive to the mall and park and buy stuff and eat in the food court. My colleague, who after two weeks was accustomed to my ways, had the grace to laugh convincingly.

That night, I wrote a poem. It is at least half composed by the students in that class—based on things they said. One day, I had started the discussion by asking them: If you could write one great poem—it would be read on television, it would go up on the walls of public buildings, people would memorize it—what would you want your poem to be about? I asked for each of them to name a subject in one or two words, like a title, and then the reasons for their choice.

My poem is based faithfully on the four student responses to that question, ending with an especially strong answer from a student who had both impaired vision and impaired hearing. Her firmly delivered words capped the discussion, as they cap my poem:

IF YOU COULD WRITE ONE GREAT POEM,
WHAT WOULD YOU WANT IT TO BE ABOUT?

(Asked of four student poets at the Illinois Schools
for the Deaf and the Visually Impaired)

Fire, because it is quick, and can destroy.
Music, place where anger has its place.
Romantic Love—the cold or stupid ask why.
Sign: that it is a language, full of grace,

That it is visible, invisible, dark and clear,
That it is loud and noiseless and is contained
Inside a body and explodes in air
Out of a body to conquer from the mind.

It was a pleasure to print out five copies of the poem, and read it aloud to our group. I was glad to be there, and I was aware that it was good fortune, given to me by the kinds of institutions I mistrust and complain about, grumpily.

XI

Hergesheimer

AFTER MY father's business began to thrive, he joined a peer group of Jersey Shore opticians. There were five or six of them, with offices in Manasquan, Asbury Park, Freehold, Red Bank and Bradley Beach. They met once a month, in somebody's living room, to discuss their work over drinks and snacks. They must have complained to one another about the ophthalmologists, those lordly M.D.s who sometimes asked opticians for kickbacks. The needs and demands of summer vacationers might have been a topic. Maybe the opticians traded tips about wholesalers or income tax.

At one of those monthly meetings one of the group noticed that the eyeglasses of another were slipping down his nose. Or maybe the frame was a bit crooked. The optician who noticed the need for an adjustment removed the frame gently from his colleague's face and while trying to correct it he snapped the thing in two. There was a lot of laughter, and of course the guy who broke the eyeglasses promised to bring a replacement, the same model of frame in the same size with the lenses inserted, to their next meeting.

A few days later, the opticians in the group learned that the one who broke his colleague's eyeglasses had been hospitalized. He was undergoing what was described as a complete nervous breakdown. The funny incident now seemed like a symptom of something wrong, deep down. For my father, it may have been all the more poignant because of his wife's concussion and his stepmother Molly's death in the state mental hospital.

To the credit of the opticians, they took turns keeping their friend's business going while he was disabled. I think well enough of my fellow poets to believe that we would do— have done—something similar, in the same kind of situation. When Harvard denied the young student Stanley Kunitz a teaching position for explicitly anti-semitic reasons, he vowed never to teach again. Years later, when Kunitz's friend Theodore Roethke suffered a mental collapse while teaching at Bennington, he recommended that to replace him the college hire Kunitz, who accepted.

In the story of the broken eyeglass frame, I'm moved and interested by the element of laughter. When the frame got broken, the opticians laughed. Denial of what just happened must have been part of the laughter: denial of the aggression along with the aggression. The group shared a firm, experienced understanding of adjusting eyeglasses, an understanding that gave them their complicated laughter, that returned in little bursts for the rest of that evening together. Easy to imagine that Kunitz and Roethke, too, laughed.

In poetry, I find a comparable kind of laughter in Stevie Smith's "Thoughts About the Person from Porlock," her debunking of Samuel Taylor Coleridge's prefatory note to his "Kubla Khan." His note explains away the fragmentary, unknowable nature of improvisation: the element of making a poem that is beyond control or preparation. Smith's poem lets me laugh at Coleridge, but kindly, allowing my fearful identification with his elaborately imagined excuse. His poem is a fragment, Coleridge explains in his note, because in mid-dream he was awakened "by a person on business from Porlock." He was dreaming the poem, he maintains, and the fragment "Kubla Khan" is an interrupted memory of the dream, not a plan or a failure. Stevie Smith responds to that with her skeptical but sympathetic version of, *Oh, yeah?* She wishes for a person from Porlock, always, to help her find an excuse when she feels stuck.

I don't have any personal story of aggression, laughter or denial as dramatic as my father's, but I can think of some milder examples. I have served as poetry editor for magazines, choosing a few poems to publish and rejecting many others. I did that for the *New Republic*, then years later for *Slate*.

At *Slate*, we published a new poem every week, and asked each poet to record their poem so *Slate* readers could hear it read aloud—a good idea, now commonplace, that was something new and strange in 1996. We actually mailed a recording device, with prepaid return packaging, to each poet. The payment for a poem was not bad, something like $250 in 1996 dollars, as I remember. For the first issues, I solicited poems from friends, including Lucille Clifton, Louise Glück, Seamus Heaney and C. K. Williams.

Back then, the concept of a magazine on the internet needed explanation. Williams was living in Paris. When he found a check in the mail from the Microsoft Corporation (*Slate*'s originator), he was bewildered. Why would Microsoft send him money? He decided Bill Gates must be sending a check to every American, as a way of keeping us all sweet.

As poetry editor, I also wrote introductions for an occasional feature we called "Classic Poems," with an introduc-

tory paragraph or two accompanying a poem by the likes of
Fulke Greville, Louise Bogan, or Robert Hayden. I read the
Classic Poem aloud, in some long-forgotten audio format, and
responded to readers' comments in "The Fray," a surprisingly rich, civilized predecessor to the troll-cursed present-
day terrain of Comments.

Sometimes, in the cover letters people enclosed with
their poetry submissions, a raging hunger for attention
exploded, tearing through the businesslike surface: the
equivalent, in a way, of destroying the eyeglasses you meant
to adjust. I wrote a parody of those letters and sent it to
Howard Moss at *The New Yorker*, where it appeared as a
"Shouts and Murmurs" piece on April 18, 1983, under the
name "Ada Johnston."

In a reversal of refusing to edit my name out of "The
Figured Wheel," I had decided to use a pseudonym for this
piece. It seemed right to avoid offending people who had submitted poems. I can't reconstruct how I arrived at the pseudonym. It concealed some kind of (now-lost) alphabetical or
punning tribute to Veronica Geng, a supremely funny prose
writer with a great ear for literary foolishness. She died young
of brain cancer a few years before I hid myself behind "Ada
Johnston."

My fictional poetry editor is named Martin Hergesheimer.
It was fun to show him victimized by the snubs, the demands
for attention and the virtual exploding cigars that might
humiliate a young poet. In Berkeley, Bob Hass and I used to
meet for coffee twice a week at the Café Renaissance, where
Hergesheimer, you could say, often joined us. Hass became
a Hergesheimer fan, and for decades now, we have used the
name in new, not entirely imaginary stories.

Say, for instance, that you are about to give a poetry reading, and while you are listening to the person introducing
you, a man seated next to you in the audience shoves a piece

of paper into your face: a poem he wrote. When you gesture toward the introducer, the guy scowls and whispers that you have plenty of time, his poem is not long, it's a sonnet—just read it. That is a Hergesheimer experience. In time, the poet Brenda Hillman introduced Ms. Hergesheimer and her similar adventures.

Hergesheimer, in his little social world of poetry, suffers the muffled aggression of various types. A senior poet writes:

Dear Mr. Hergesheimer:

Enclosed please find a poem, "The Pangs of Silenus," submitted for publication in *The National Monthly*, and return envelope.

It might interest you to know that this would be my first publication in *TNM* since some forty years ago, when the poetry editor was the late C. Bradley Flemming, that lovable old scoundrel and crypto-Trotskyite. Before I fell afoul of him, Chuck wrote me a letter in which he called my early poem "The Nausea of Narcissus: An Ode," ". . . the most searching lyric of its kind that our generation has yet produced."

Well, he was a strange man, and an unspeakably ugly drunk, but a fine critic. We won't see his like again.

Good wishes to you in your work.

> Yours truly,
> Edward Cabot Cooper

Another of Ada Johnston's creations wrote to Hergesheimer:

I enclose for your consideration the opening five sections
of my narrative poem "Nostradamus," constituting
Volume One of a projected twelve-volume narrative of
Nostradamus's life. I realize that the entire Volume may
be a bit long for TNM's format. (But only a page or two
longer than that—I thought—prolix elegy by Ashby
Wickes that you recently printed, however.) If length
is a problem, I would be willing for the poem to be
serialized. Or it could be excerpted as follows:

Sections 2 and 3, followed by the first hundred and
fifty lines of Section 5 (through the line "The drear
saliva of the Saracen maw"), retitled "Earth, Angels,
and Astronauts." Another possibility would be to print
Section 5, in its entirety and with its present title,
followed by Section 1. Or do you feel that the material in
Section 2, about Nostradamus's second marriage, is too
essential to cut?

The footnotes—though perhaps helpful to readers
unfamiliar with such material as the Plague of 1547, the
rather bizarre intrigues of the Court, or the *Scientific
American* article cited in Section 4—are optional.

Even if you decide that *TNM* is not the right place for
the poem, I look forward eagerly to your response. I have
read your new book, and was particularly interested by
your poem "Meadow," since my book *Pasteur: A Poem*
contains a longish passage about a pasture. I will have
my publisher, Cold Calm Press, send you a review copy.

Sincerely yours,
Patrick Cutwarp

I'll cite one more of the (mostly) fictional contributors:

Dear Hergesheimer,

I thought that *The National Monthly* might be interested
in publishing my poem

   "t   t / t   t"
    a   o   u   s
    u   n   n   a
    r   s   a   o
    o -   - r

The printer should photograph the poem directly from
the enclosed copy of my typescript.

Cheers,
sTen tOrnquist

These exaggerated versions of poetry correspondence
belong in the category of office jokes. The self-importance of
poets is no funnier and no more meaningful than the poses
affected by beauticians, orthopedists or cheesemakers. Examples include the competitive, small-minded English clergymen
in Anthony Trollope's *Barchester Towers* and the competitive,
small-minded ballplayers of Jim Bouton's *Ball Four*.

Hergesheimer, I could hope, gave me a way of laughing at
myself.

XXII

And Another Thing

THERE'S A theory that the human species evolved depression over hundreds of thousands of years as a useful spur to new ideas. My lifelong habit of muttering aloud to myself, sometimes in single words like "*stupid*" or "*death*" or just "*no*": that incantation of self-disappointment isn't exactly depression, I think, but more like a generalized "I should-have-done" or "I-should-have-said."

An example: In the question period after a poetry reading, someone in the audience rose to say the musicality had been impressive, but particularly striking was how distinctly I pronounced the words. The consonants in particular, that person said, seemed not characteristic of American speech or art. American speech is quite slurred. What does it mean, sir, that your approach is so different from that?

I don't remember how I responded, but I do remember that it wasn't very good. Maybe I constructed some wordy version of "Everybody is different." But I do know what I wish I had done: maybe just pronounce two or three names.

Nat "King" Cole. Ella Fitzgerald. Frank Sinatra. Nina Simone. Hank Williams. The classic American singers I had heard all my life, since I was an infant, on the radio or on records. Gene Autry—maybe his way with words as he sang them formed my idea of sentence melodies and rhythms. The same for the elegant phrasing of Joe Williams. Annie Ross. Bing Crosby. The Mills Brothers. The Platters. In their different ways, they all convey a boundless, audible joy in distinct articulation of consonant and vowel. Sinatra's expressive diction, New Jersey accent and all, I could have pointed out, is precise.

Or, I could have recommended the diction of "Little Richard" Penniman on his recording of "Send Me Some Lovin'." Even in the most legato, improvised passages, every syllable is distinct. Aretha Franklin's mastery of consonants carving vowels might have led me to her father, the great preacher C. L. Franklin, and the tradition of American sermon eloquence, Black and white.

The sermon eloquence, with its staccato consonants shaping the croon of the vowels, informs the tradition of political eloquence. I could have mentioned famous speeches, or even the percussion of consonants in the diction of Umar Bin Hassen in the Last Poets' famous track "When the Revolution Comes." Is the pronunciation of the great stand-up comics slurred? Does the super-articulate Darth Vader not have an American accent?

But no. I blathered something or other with, as I recall, not much content. I wish I had said simply, with examples, that there is a great, popular, distinctly American tradition of precise consonants and vowels.

Why did the ability to improvise fail me? Maybe the effort of keeping a cool surface got in the way. The performer's motto "Never let them see you sweat" infected me early in life. On occasions like that Q&A, straining to stay—or appear—cool can disable me. I heard a critique of how I pronounce words, and inside my armor it made me sweat. The motto about what you never let them see may be good for performance, but sometimes it is bad for public relations. The armor can appear complacent.

Or the dogma can turn inward, and become: "Don't let yourself know you're sweating." I remember, a very long time ago, an envelope with the return address of an institution that would decide my future for the coming year. Did they grant me the money to live on? The answer was in that envelope, so—those who know me best will understand—I felt compelled to display it on a mantel, visible and unopened, for a week, as though to show the envelope, or the committee it represented—or myself—that I was above any concern over what it contained.

About not mentioning Ella Fitzgerald or Gene Autry, my regret is more than pure esprit d'escalier. (The French is suitable for the feeling.) That little failure is worth muttering, "No," over because it fell short of a larger, heartfelt point: that art in a democracy can soar beyond categories of "high" and "low." The art of poetry has sometimes been regarded as a ruling class property—and in theory the ruling class in the United States is the people. I had let down, or at least neglected, an idea that was important to me.

It would have been too much to tell the story of Paul Fussell's war experiences, or the murder of Henry Dumas, or my father's essay on being a gentleman. But why didn't those stories inspire me at least a little toward asking the questioner if she had ever heard (maybe on YouTube?) Eartha Kitt pronounce the double *tt* in her name?

Closer to home, among the American singers in my own generation, I wish I had mentioned Lee Andrews, the father of Questlove and celebrated in my poem "The Hearts" that I quite likely read aloud that same night. I could have said . . . But I have gone on (and on) about that moment long enough.

Another little failure, of a different kind: When our kids

were small, Ellen and I stole away from Berkeley for a weekend hiking in the mountains known as the Trinity Alps, north of Weaverville. Under the California sky, I now and then quoted poems I liked enough to have by memory. Elizabeth Bishop and William Carlos Williams. Shakespeare. And certainly William Butler Yeats.

Of course, I misquoted a lot. That's part of the pleasure in memorizing. And mistakes are instructive. As in sports or music, getting something a bit wrong can electrify a practice session and propel your technique to innovation. In a situation like two people hiking through magnificent country, what's the harm if you approach a poem just a little bit the way performers approach a folk song or the words of a traditional blues?

I had a short poem by Yeats pretty accurately by heart, except for one word in the fourth line:

ON BEING ASKED FOR A WAR POEM

> I think it better that in times like these
> A poet's mouth be silent, for in truth
> We have no gift to set a statesman right;
> He has had enough of [*something*] who can please
> A young girl in the indolence of her youth,
> Or an old man upon a winter's night.

The first time I tried to speak the poem, there on the mountain, I said, "He has had enough of *glory*" . . . But that did not sound right, Ellen and I agreed.

You could argue for "glory." As somewhat stereotypical characters, the young girl and the old man represent people who have on their mind things other than poetry. To please unlikely readers, as if by surprise, might be a stroke of glory. And there's a good contrast with a more conventional use of "glory," given that "war" is in the poem's title. But such case-making is a stretch. The word just doesn't work very well.

We talked it over as we climbed the trail, and after a while Ellen had a suggestion we both decided was better than "glory":

> He has had enough of *striving* who can please
> A young girl in the indolence of her youth,
> Or an old man upon a winter's night.

"Striving" makes more sense than "glory." It is in the right key for a poem where the girl feels lazy and the old man feels cold. It also is better than "glory" for declining a request. But "striving" is flat. It doesn't add much more thought or feeling than the placeholder "something."

We kept trying off and on for another two or three hours, and I could not find the right word in a poem I had read many times over many years. I knew enough to know that the word was there in the poem, and that I had not found it. That frustration propelled my marvel at the poem—and at precise, poetic meaning itself.

As soon as we came off the mountain, I needed to find a bookstore. Weaverville (to the town's glory) had a store with a volume of Yeats on its shelves. I bought the book, as seemed right. But first I turned to the page where I could find what the master had written and I could not remember.

The word that Yeats actually uses in his poem is tougher, meaner, more harshly resistant—and in a way dismissive—than anything we had come up with. There it was on the page, kind of shocking:

ON BEING ASKED FOR A WAR POEM

> I think it better that in times like these
> A poet's mouth be silent, for in truth

> We have no gift to set a statesman right;
> He has had enough of meddling who can please
> A young girl in the indolence of her youth,
> Or an old man upon a winter's night.

There in Weaverville, along with my surprise, pleasure and chagrin at finding the word, I realized that "meddling" made me think about the poem's historical context. The war in question is World War I, about which a poet from the colonized nation of Ireland might feel ambivalent. The long history of Ireland's treatment by the British Empire included mass killing and starvation, along with prolonged and ingenious forms of humiliation. In another poem by Yeats of the same period, "An Irish Airman Foresees His Death," the airman of the title says, "Those that I fight I do not hate, / Those that I guard I do not love."

Beyond that political background, Yeats had provided me a lesson in creative writing as well as history. The word "meddling" gives an audacious rightness to the action of this particular poem, and to its fabric. In his poems "Easter 1916" and "Meditations in Time of Civil War," "meddling" would be all wrong to describe poetic striving for something larger (or more glorious?) than simply to please.

The Variorum Edition of the Poems of W. B. Yeats tells me that in early versions of "On Being Asked for a War Poem," the second line did not say it was better that "A poet's mouth be silent" but that "We poets keep our mouths shut"—all the more daringly rude, and more dismissive, but not as good. The master knew what he was doing.

That day, the poem also gave me a specific, indelible lesson about the cheap sweetness I may too easily dismiss as "sentimental"—a loose, all-purpose term. "Meddling" in Yeats's fifty-two-word poem sets an example. Plausible nice poetry tells lies. If it fibs about how benign the natural world is, or how benign the author is, then it disables the truth-seeking missile that guided the Irish poet to "meddling" in a poem that declines an imperial invitation. Far different, in that same historical setting, is "Easter 1916," with its refrain that "A terrible beauty is born." The dark, tormented nature of that beauty, in the specific realm of Irish history, is different in another way from the wide gaze of the poem I typed and pasted on my kitchen wall in college: "What is past, and passing, and to come."

"Sailing to Byzantium" brings me to another regret, also in response to a questioner, this time about an anthology I published a couple of years ago: *The Mind Has Cliffs of Fall: Poems at the Extremes of Feeling.* In the paperback, it was retitled *The Book of Poetry for Hard Times.* The chapters include "The Sleep of Reason," "Grief," "Love and Rage," "Guilt, Shame, Blame" and "Despair."

At a public reading from that book, someone in the audience asked me about the section titled "Despair." Might I consider someday making an anthology with a section of poems under the title "Hope"?

"No," I said too quickly. "Hope is boring."

That glib answer was funny for a moment, but it was impolite, and another blown opportunity to say something better. Again, the pose of not sweating led to bad personal politics.

I could have said that the English word "despair" is built from the French word for hope. Elizabeth Bishop makes a kind of joke on that word-origin in her "Crusoe in England," with "the volcano / I'd christened *Mont d'Espoir* or *Mount Despair.*" That might have made the point, politely, that poems about despair are poems about hope.

Since this retrospective improvement on "Hope is boring" is a fantasy anyway, I'll imagine myself quoting Geoffrey Chaucer's line in "The Parson's Tale": "Now cometh wanhope that is despair of the mercy of god." The sin of wanhope—weak faith—is the theme of the poem by Gerard Manley Hopkins that gave me the anthology's title, *The Mind Has Cliffs of Fall*. (Later, *The Book of Poetry for Hard Times*.)

The poems under that anthology's heading of "Despair" all involve hope and its absence. Those "Despair" poems, arranged historically, range from Dante through Emily Dickinson ("The Difference Between Despair and Fear") and Thomas Hardy ("Some blessed Hope of which he knew, / And I was unaware") to contemporary poems by Tracy Smith ("We dwindle by the day"), Maggie Dietz ("Who wants to be that kind of happy"), and Rowan Ricardo Phillips ("It does not get you quite wrong.") Any one of those poems can be understood as a unique chapter in the history of wanhope, which is also the history of hope.

And the history of regret is also the history of aspiration. What I wish I had said becomes another form of ambition, and at least some willingness to try again even though, as Yeats says, "A living man is blind and drinks his drop. / What matter if the ditches are impure."

In that same late poem, "A Dialogue of Self and Soul," he writes a dreary summary of his life and asks, weirdly, if he'd be willing to live it over again:

> What matter if I live it all once more?
> Endure that toil of growing up;
> The ignominy of boyhood; the distress
> Of boyhood changing into man;
> The unfinished man and his pain
> Brought face to face with his own clumsiness.

"Clumsiness" makes me think of those questions I could have handled better. After that painful line, as if he's not been grim enough, Yeats goes on to:

> The finished man among his enemies?—
> How in the name of Heaven can he escape
> The defiling and disfigured shape
> The mirror of malicious eyes
> Casts upon his eyes until at last
> He thinks that shape must be his shape?

Not only will people generate nasty, unkind, distorted visions of you and your work—you will begin to think that the "mirror of malicious eyes" must be right! "*Stupid*," you might say aloud to yourself.

At least he cheers himself up at the end:

> I am content to follow to its source
> Every event in action or in thought;
> Measure the lot; forgive myself the lot!
> When such as I cast out remorse
> So great a sweetness flows into the breast
> We must laugh and we must sing,
> We are blest by everything,
> Everything we look upon is blest.

Every reader is free, on every reading of these lines, to understand the words "such as I" in different ways. And some readers will find the concept of casting out remorse unlikely, or hard to understand. For me, now, Yeats's lines feel like saying out loud to yourself, afloat in the currents of wanhope and regret: "What the Hell, it would be a great feeling—sweet, a blessing—to bring even *this* into poetry."

XXIII

The Favorite Poem Project

AN INSIDE joke at the Poet Laureate's office in Washington was a variation on the acronym POTUS to indicate the President of the United States. People referred to the poet as PLOTUS, sometimes pronounced aloud, as in "the Plotus will say a few words."

Soon after she was appointed PLOTUS, Louise Glück got a letter denouncing her. The letter writer, Louise told me, scolded her for accepting the position while acknowledging, in interviews, that she did not intend to do the kind of public works undertaken by some of her predecessors, such as Rita Dove, Robert Hass, and Robert Pinsky.

"How dare you accept the taxpayer's money," said the letter, "without working for it?"

I explained to the PLOTUS that her critic was mistaken: the modest annual stipend does not come from tax dollars, but from a private endowment, established long ago by the Huntington family.

"Oh, too late," said Louise. "I already mailed the guy a five-dollar bill with a note, 'Dear Mr. So-and-so, here's your refund.'"

As to public works, Rita had created a program exploring the African diaspora, and fostered creative writing programs in D.C.'s public schools. Bob had arranged a conference at the Library of Congress bringing together literary writers on nature with more scientific writers on ecology.

So what about me?

What did I care about? Did I have a project about Jewish guys from New Jersey? No. (Or not exactly.) But maybe my thinking did cleave to a particular Jewish tradition of universalizing? For example, when a national poetry organization sent poets into city high schools and libraries to discuss a great poet, they suggested that I speak about the work of Yehuda Amichai. I responded that Amichai was a great poet, I loved his work, but I would rather talk about Emily Dickinson.

Was that choice in the same tradition that made Herbert, Milton and Sidney become Jewish first names? Was it related to some Jewish "cosmopolitan" quality? Whatever it's called, could a willingness to adopt or adapt have exacerbated the anti-semitism of that art school reject Adolf Hitler? A cosmopolitan tradition—hopeful and omnivorous and integrative—may have guided my thinking about a national project.

A few years earlier, I had published an op-ed essay about memorized poetry. "Any room full of Americans," I wrote, "has more poetry in it than each separate person in the room may suppose, in their combined memories."

A crowded elevator of people, I suggested, might collaborate to improvise an interesting anthology. It would likely include poems by William Shakespeare, Emily Dickinson and Robert Frost, along with naughty limericks and lyrics by Cole Porter, Johnny Mercer, Fats Waller, Joni Mitchell, David Bowie and Leonard Cohen. I mentioned Robert Creeley's short poem "I Know a Man," which some people in my generation had by heart. I told about a Berkeley creative writing class, a group that included people from the East and South as well as California. There was a Black man from D.C. in the class, and a woman from the Philippines. Everyone in the group of a dozen people had memorized the opening lines of Geoffrey Chaucer's "Prologue" to *The Canterbury Tales*. Two or three people in the class, helping one another, could continue reciting the "Prologue" beyond those opening lines. One way or another, people have more poetry in them than you might think, I proposed.

I began to think about a PLOTUS project demonstrating not only that Americans know more poetry than you might assume—but that many of them care deeply for the art. The Laureate office is at the Library of Congress, in the heart of D.C. We could interview tourists waiting in line to tour the White House, the Capitol, the Supreme Court and other Washington attractions. We could ask them what poetry they liked, or maybe had a bit of by heart, and make recordings of the responses.

David Gewanter, the poet teaching at Georgetown, liked the idea, and he is not shy. Helping with an early Favorite Poem reading at the Library of Congress, David went into a D.C. police station and asked at the desk if there were any officers there who liked poetry. The desk officer immediately referred David to an officer who, at the Favorite Poem reading, recited Thomas Hardy's "The Work Box" (a poem about a crime) very effectively, in a Georgia accent.

At that same reading where the police officer read Hardy's poem, and a ninth-grader read one by Emily Dickinson, two United States senators, John Kerry of Massachusetts and Thad Cochran of Mississippi, both chose to read Robert Frost's poem "The Road Not Taken." Their remarks about the poem were strikingly different—in fact, opposite in exactly the ways to be expected from a Democrat and a Republican of their time.

In the late nineties, the Clinton administration was looking for ways to celebrate the new millennium. A young administrator at the National Endowment for the Arts, Cliff Becker, attended that reading with the police officer reading Hardy, the junior high school student reading Dickinson and the two senators reading Frost.

In ways I still don't understand, Becker managed to make the Favorite Poem Project a fulfillment of the Clinton administration's desire for millennial programs. The FPP created a video portrait of the United States in 2000, through the lens not of politics or entertainment or professional sports, but the enduring, surprisingly vigorous, in its way universal medium of poetry.

By filming Americans at home and at work, or any place they felt at ease, the project combined something like the appeal of gossip with the appeal of art: unique human faces and voices, each person in their different setting, saying poems by the likes of William Shakespeare, Arthur Rimbaud, Pablo Neruda or Gwendolyn Brooks. Personally, I found a hidden doorway leading away from the failure-haunted corridors of getting a D for Citizenship.

With a budget and plans for a video archive, the Favorite Poem Project made a public call for volunteers, looking for serious poetry readers with a wide range of regional accents, ages, ethnicities, professions and kinds of education. The videos and the anthologies that emerged present an art project that is in an unusual, actual way, public, based visibly and at its core on readers—"the public"—rather than on artists or experts.

Public, but not dumbed-down or (on the other hand) academic. By concentrating on individual readers, we avoided the more familiar kinds of poetry video that presented poets, critics, or actors. The video segments, with portraits of readers responding to poems and reading them aloud, were shown on PBS. Quotations from readers' letters introduced the poems in the anthology, *Americans' Favorite Poems*. In that title, the apostrophe after the plural is important. The poems are the choices of particular people, not an aggregate but a plural, not a statistical poll but a documentary collection. And neither show business nor school.

In one of the first video segments, the U.S. Marine Steve Conteaguero reads William Butler Yeats's poem "Politics." He cogently relates Yeats's poem to elements in his own life: his military service, his Cuban American family's political history, and above all his marriage, the most central, personal element, and the least political, he explains.

In another video, Pov Chin, a high school student in San Jose, reads the poem "Minstrel Man" by Langston Hughes. As the Marine does with Yeats's "Politics," she reads Hughes's poem twice, near the beginning of the video and again at the end. Throughout the video, her mother remains seated in the background, watchful throughout. In her comments, Pov Chin relates "Minstrel Man" to her family's ordeal, when she was an infant, fleeing the nightmare of the Pol Pot years.

"They split us up," she says of the Khmer Rouge who divided the family, with a striking first-person plural: Pov Chin was in her mother's womb when the soldiers killed two of the family's children, her brothers, and her grandmother. The video briefly includes a photograph of the murdered grandmother, along with other family pictures, arranged in a living room shrine. After her remarks about Hughes's poem, Pov Chin reads it the second time. The poem is in sixteen short lines, and the video takes less than five minutes. The effect is in a way epic.

"Epic" is defined by Ezra Pound as "a poem containing history." The first-person plural of "They split us up" expresses family feeling in relation to the large, catastrophic forces of war, politics, national identities. The Cambodian family's story reaches from colonialism and the Khmer Rouge to that living room in San Jose, with the shrine and the watchful mother, with Pov Chin's American voice and her first-person plural. That story contains history.

Maybe the best-known of the Favorite Poem Project videos is a Whitman segment where John Doherty, a construction worker for the Boston power company, reads lines from "Leaves of Grass." We see him at work. He says that his admiration for Whitman does not depend mainly on the poem's celebration of working people. What matters to him, Doherty says, is some hard-to-define spirit in the poetry. He thanks Whitman for encouraging persistence—the poem dealing directly, explicitly, with the truth that a reader will likely not understand all of a poem the first time. He reads Whitman's lines with an understated assurance:

> The spotted hawk swoops by and accuses me . . . he
>   complains of my gab and my loitering.
>
> I too am not a bit tamed . . . I too am untranslatable,
> I sound my barbaric yawp over the roofs of the world.

After this Whitman video appeared on the *PBS NewsHour*, John Doherty received a number of fan letters, some of them commenting on how attractive he looked in his hard hat and uniform.

At a social gathering related to the FPP, I met John Doherty (in suit and necktie). We chatted, and I asked him if he took much teasing and ridicule from his colleagues at work because of the poetry video, given the television showing and the Favorite Poem Project website. Did they mock him?

"You have no idea how much crap I take," he said. And then, with a little smile, "But women like it."

Recently, the Favorite Poem Project has added two more videos of people reading poetry by Walt Whitman. The Chinese filmmaker and writer Xu Xing reads from Whitman's "Song of the Open Road" in the Mandarin translation he first encountered as a teenager, during the Cultural Revolution. He tells the story of how he fell in love with a certain classmate. Trying to impress the young woman, he sent her an ardent note, writing to her not about love, but about human freedom—and the American poet Walt Whitman. She immediately gave the note to their teacher, who was also a police agent. The teacher-officer at once put Xu Xing under arrest, giving the young poetry lover and future filmmaker his first experience of trouble with the authorities.

In a third Whitman segment, Mike Eruzione, captain of the United States hockey team that won the 1980 Olympics "Miracle on Ice" match against the Soviet Union, reads Whitman's "O Captain, My Captain!" The choice of poem may seem a corny or vulgar play on the word "captain"—Eruzione's role on the historic hockey team. As he says in the video, the word is a coincidence. He heard Whitman's poem many times for years, beginning when he was a small child. At family gatherings in Winchester, Massachusetts, family members would call for Mike's father to recite "O Captain, My Captain!" It was a set-piece performance in Eruzione family tradition. The celebrated Olympics hero explains on camera that he cannot read "O Captain, My Captain!" as dramatically as did his father, who emphasized certain lines with an audience-pleasing drama. Mike Eruzione reads the poem in a less theatrical way, bringing to Whitman's lines an amused celebration of his beloved, hambone father reading the same lines to family cheers and applause.

The process of recruiting readers for the videos and anthologies was homemade. Cards left in libraries and bookstores, or reprinted in magazines, asked people to write a few sentences about a poem they liked. With no advertising budget, we received eighteen thousand submissions. Fewer people had access to email back in 2000, and there was not yet a Favorite Poem Project website. The submissions mostly came by mail to a Boston University address.

I had never done anything like this project before. My predecessor, Bob Hass, told me I needed to ask Boston University for a part-time graduate assistant, to handle phone calls and mail. So in her early twenties the poet Maggie Dietz became director of the Favorite Poem Project—an organizing producer for the videos and editor of the anthologies.

She also set up the Favorite Poem reading at the White House, with months of telephone conferences, mail and faxes. The Clinton administration aides and officials had no idea they were dealing with somebody so young. A Washington and Martha's Vineyard hostess told me, "I tried for years to arrange a White House event like this and I never made it. But *Maggie Dietz* made it happen"—as though she were talking about a powerful lobbyist. (For the event, Maggie's mother and father bought her a suit.)

At the White House reading, with an audience including poets from all over the United States, Bill Clinton read Ralph Waldo Emerson's "Concord Hymn." Hillary Clinton read Howard Nemerov's poem about poets, "The Makers." Rita Dove, Robert Hass and I read poems by Emily Dickinson, Walt Whitman, E. A. Robinson, Robert Frost, Robert Hayden, Gwendolyn Brooks and William Carlos Williams. A disabled veteran read, from his wheelchair, Frost's poem with "But I have promises to keep" followed by the repeated line "And miles to go before I sleep." At the after party, President Clinton discussed foreign policy with John Ashbery and Rita Dove. He knew that Caroline Pinsky was a veterinarian, so he took our family to meet Buddy, the Clinton family dog.

More complicated than that evening, and more prolonged, was producing the videos. Maggie organized BU student interns at computers to create a digital database, typing out entries from many thousands of postcards and letters on paper that became files. We narrowed down those files to several hundred possibilities and finally to the fifty segments that got made. Executive producer Juanita Anderson, who also shot some of the segments, knew how to squeeze the best product out of the least money. She knew expert regional filmmakers all over the United States, and brought them together in Boston to design the project, so we did not have to fly a crew all over the country. With a budget of $500,000, Juanita produced more than 250 minutes of memorable video, with high production values.

The poems chosen for the videos and for the anthologies Norton published do not necessarily reflect my taste or Juanita's or Maggie's—but they do reflect our editorial standards. Whitman and Dickinson must be included. Rod McKuen, Rupi Kaur or others in the Edgar Guest tradition, no. The approach was egalitarian in some ways, and in other ways elitist. As to debates about the validity of taste, good pizza is better than bad pizza, though the bad pizza place may have its followers. I trusted my standards, and up to a point I suspended my taste.

There were decisions regarding the choice of readers, from their letters. If the reason for liking a poem was, "My high school teacher Miss Cooper used to read it to us, and she had great legs," that was a laugh but probably a "no." Better: "On our second date, my husband and I discovered we both had this poem by heart"—we were interested. In a memorable letter, the writer said she first encountered Pablo Neruda's "Tonight I Can Write" as a teenager, when the poem was sent to her by a boy who copied it out longhand and claimed he wrote it. The boy was forgotten, but the plagiarized poem by Neruda stayed with her.

For the book's italicized headnotes on the poems, we got permission to make brief excerpts from what people had written. This is the entire note on Jane Kenyon's poem "Otherwise":

> *I live with cancer. I know there is an otherwise.*
> —Jamien Morehouse, 48, Artist, Rockport, Maine

After *Americans' Favorite Poems* was published, we got a letter from Jamien Morehouse's husband. She had died in the interim, and until the book appeared he had no idea that she had chosen Kenyon's poem and written to us. He thanked us for adding to his memories of her.

Personal and civic, the Favorite Poem Project is based on a sense of poetry as older and more primary than prose and closely related to music, in a place distinct from both show business and academia: an American public space for the art of poetry, and for the voice of its audience.

XXIV

Immigrant Paths

P LYMOUTH COLONY and Jamestown were European colonies populated by immigrants from England, the Netherlands, and Scotland. In a notably different pattern, the colony of New Jersey was populated by American immigrants from those other colonies and New York. A second wave. That bit of history fits with the idea that New Jersey is somehow the most immigrant state. It offers good Syrian food, or Dominican, for example.

Or do I mean the most American state, in a certain, biased sense?

Marvin Hagler, possibly the most admirable pure fighter in the history of boxing, was originally from Newark, the same city where my grandfather Dave began in life as a young tough guy. Hagler is deeply associated with Brockton, Massachusetts, the city of Rocky Marciano. Like Newark, a blue-collar place. In Brockton, Hagler became a protégé, student and lifelong friend of the brothers Pat and Goody Petronelli, boxing experts, respectively manager and trainer.

Reading Hagler's obituary, I thought of Yvor Winters and his interest in the sport, and of the grandfather who every year gave me boxing gloves for my birthday. Maybe he gave me two pairs, or else he gave the same present to my bratty cousin Joey. The family men staged a bout when Joey and I were ten or eleven years old. Joey was what used to be called "spoiled." When he charged at me pinwheeling his arms madly, I decided to show my superiority by holding out one glove stiff-arm and letting him run into it. The tactic worked. Joey ran crashing into my motionless fist so hard, face-first, the impact knocked him down.

But instead of the praise I anticipated for my high-class cool, Zaydee Pop delivered what might be called my first disappointing review.

"The kid," said my grandfather, smiling down at Joey, "can take a punch."

I don't mean to endorse that ritual contest, so typical of the men who staged it, their place and their time, but I do wish I had taken the opportunity to clobber Joey. Maybe I should have learned something, sooner, from my grandfather's remark. Like the Petronelli brothers and Hagler in their way, and like Winters in his different way, Dave Pinsky knew what he was talking about. I wish he had given me more of a break. Or maybe he did give me a break I didn't understand at the time. If you are going to fight, don't pose for your portrait on a postage stamp—fight.

In the slogan presented to generations of immigrants from every continent, the United States is a land of opportunity. Along with opportunity, and maybe extending beyond it, I'd like to add another idea, though I don't have a name for it. I mean the bits of help or goodwill that may come not from some national or tribal group of your own, and not from organizations or parishes, but something on a neighborhood level, almost casual and not quite arbitrary. The impulsive luxury of giving somebody a break.

Reaching for an instance, I think of that small-town police

officer who locks up a kid caught shoplifting, then lets him go after a few hours, to teach him a lesson. He chooses to give the child—not necessarily of the same ethnic category as the cop, though probably white—a break. The break may lead to something good, or be appreciated, by somebody, some time. In the spirit of local pride, I'll call it a Jersey break, and speculate that it may nourish our country's immigrant-based variety.

Or do I sentimentalize the police officer? A Black or Puerto Rican kid might not have gotten that break. It would be more likely if the Black kid's surname was known—if he was a Weaver or a Dupree—in that flawed, small-town way, or the way the country itself is flawed, in its perpetual struggle to hold itself together. The break all the more likely if the particular Weaver or Dupree's name was known from the high school's football team. But talent, like names, cuts more than one way. You have three strikes against you, Joe Frazier is quoted as telling Marvin Hagler, who had trouble getting lucrative matches: you're Black, you're left-handed, and you're good at what you do.

In the Favorite Poem Project, the variety of readers, the variety of poems, the unpredictable quality of who would select what poem—all, I believe, express an elegant, embracing weirdness in American culture. The videos often present social and political realities: immigration, slavery, public education, wars, languages. Presenting indictment and shame along with plenty to admire, the project is, in a hopeful, unresolved sense of the word, patriotic.

Underlying the assumption that there are lots of people in our country who love great poems there is a kind of covert haughtiness along with an egalitarian optimism. The idea of a democratic culture where great poetry appeals to many readers, like my father's interest in the word "gentleman," is aspirational.

The vowels voice their torrent for the shaping consonants to engage endlessly in jets, pools, channels and surges of meaning, in whoever's voice. The videos make me recall Ralph Ellison's distinction about ancestors and relatives. When Pov Chin reads Langston Hughes's "Minstrel Man" she chooses him as her ancestor as he helps her think about Cambodia.

The reader Michael Lythgoe, a veteran of the war in Vietnam, is probably about the same age as Yusef Komunyakaa. Although he lived in Washington, D.C., Lythgoe had avoided the Memorial Wall until he agreed to be filmed reading Komunyakaa's poem there, for an unforgettable FPP video. Lythgoe had chosen his contemporary and fellow veteran Komunyakaa as an ancestor, as the Jamaican immigrant Seph Rodney chose Sylvia Plath—commenting explicitly, in another great segment, on the many differences between himself and Plath.

In many other videos, of course, the ancestor is also in Ellison's figurative sense of the two words, "a relative." The Connecticut high school teacher Glaisma Perez-Silva gives a powerful reading, in English and in Spanish, of Julia de Burgos's poem "Ay, Ay, Ay de la Grifa Negra." In the video, we see Perez-Silva interact with her students, many of them (but not all) Spanish-speaking and Black. Glaisma, their teacher, explains that she stayed in Connecticut, rather than returning to her birthplace Puerto Rico, because of her mission among these her students. The video is one of my favorites partly because it shows how much stronger de Burgos's poem is in the Spanish original than in the excellent English translation by Jack Agüeros.

It was important for an American poetry project to include some poems written in languages other than English, some native for the reader, and some acquired. Dawn Hannaham of D.C. reads Aleksandr Blok's "The Night, the Street, the

Streetlamp" in what I'm told is an excellent Russian accent, acquired as a student. Lyn Aye, a medical doctor in California, reads "The Way of the Water-Hyacinth" by the Burmese poet Zawgee, who had been a friend of Lyn Aye's family. In the video, Lyn Aye comments on the water-hyacinth, in its persistent vitality, as an embodiment of the Burmese people and their languages, resisting powerful, hostile forces. In *Americans' Favorite Poems*, the order is alphabetical, so Zawgee ends the volume, coming after William Butler Yeats, Sone no Yoshitada and Adam Zagajewski.

Dr. Lyn Aye's headnote for "The Way of the Water-Hyacinth," explaining why he selected it, is well written in an alliterative way that deserves to be called poetic:

> Because of its bent, its bite. Because it's Burmese,
> because it's Buddhist, because it's beautiful.

In one of the more recent videos, health-care worker Emilio Aponte-Sierra identifies himself as a refugee. He chooses to read Antonio Machado's "Caminante, no hay camino." Explaining his attachment to that poem, Aponte-Sierra acknowledges that he did not come to the United States because he dreamed of coming here. Right-wing forces in Colombia threatened his life, because of his work with poor rural people there, so he became a refugee—hoping to catch a break. At the end of the video, he relates the poem to his own, personal understanding of "the American dream": not to be rich or successful, but to start from zero and "make my own path." And to stay alive. Emilio Aponte-Sierra, near the end of the video, reads Machado's poem in Spanish:

> *Caminante, son tus huellas*
> *el camino y nada más;*
> *Caminante, no hay camino,*

> *se hace camino al andar.*
> *Al andar se hace el camino,*
> *y al volver la vista atrás*
> *se ve la senda que nunca*
> *se ha de volver a pisar.*
> *Caminante, no hay camino*
> *sino estelas en la mar.*

We hear him read these words while we see him walk on a Florida beach with a man he loves. In the closing words of the video, he tells us that every time he reads Machado's poem, he finds something new. Earlier in the segment, near the beginning, he reads the poem in a good English translation by Mary G. Berg and Dennis Maloney:

> Traveler, your footprints
> are the only road, nothing else.
> Traveler, there is no road;
> you make your own path as you walk.
> As you walk, you make your own road,
> and when you look back
> you see the path
> you will never travel again.
> Traveler, there is no road;
> only a ship's wake on the sea.

Of course, the English words "traveler" and "road" with their separate roots cannot convey the poetic effect of "caminante" and "camino." That fact is in the nature of poetry, and of languages, and of these two specific languages. Spanish, in Machado's poem, uses the single root "caminar" for the road and the traveler; English, the tongue of a much-invaded island, then of an empire, combines different roots in the translation of the poem. "Traveler" reaches back to the Anglo-Norman speech of the oppressive conquerors of

Ivanhoe, the novel and movie that impressed me when I was a child. "Road," with its Germanic-Scandinavian roots, comes from the language of Walter Scott's noble underdogs the Saxons, including Ivanhoe, who protected the Jew Isaac of Monmouth, and his beautiful daughter, played by Elizabeth Taylor.

The vowels and consonants, and the different sentence-shapes of meaning: all are unique, and unique each time. Each language, each person, each voice each time it speaks, has a different adaptive, history-saturated character. The Colombian public health official Emilio Aponte-Sierra fled to the United States to save his life. Different though he and I are in many ways, we both appreciate Antonio Machado's poem, written in the language Aponte-Sierra knew from birth and that I studied with my teacher, football coach Armando Ippolito, the child of Italian immigrants and a classmate of Sylvia Pinsky's, the child of immigrants from Poland and Romania.

These connections—by language and blood, by exile, desperation, chance and hallowed custom, forgotten or remembered—can be denied or affirmed, or both and all, as I attempt in my poem "Samurai Song," inspired by a Japanese poem I heard at a Favorite Poem reading in Kansas. The poem in its way denies need but makes a catalogue of needs.

Absence can be a form of presence, is the idea:

SAMURAI SONG

When I had no roof I made
Audacity my roof. When I had
No supper my eyes dined.

When I had no eyes I listened.
When I had no ears I thought.
When I had no thought I waited.

When I had no father I made
Care my father. When I had
No mother I embraced order.

When I had no friend I made
Quiet my friend. When I had no
Enemy I opposed my body.

When I had no temple I made
My voice my temple. I have
No priest, my tongue is my choir.

When I have no means fortune
Is my means. When I have
Nothing, death will be my fortune.

Need is my tactic, detachment
Is my strategy. When I had
No lover I courted my sleep

You may proclaim independence by invoking dependence in its different forms, from parents, through temple and choir, to the lover. And to the end. As you continue on your way through presences and absences, you make a path to your destination. When you look back, you can see the path you will never travel again: a subsiding marker like the wake of a ship.

ACKNOWLEDGMENTS

I'M GRATEFUL FOR the insight, encouragement and candor of Jeffrey Brown, Jay Cantor, Louis Chude-Sokei, Susan Davis, Maggie Dietz, Stuart Dischell, Tom Farber, Annette Frost, Jonathan Galassi, Louise Glück, Stephen Greenblatt, Robert Hass, Edward Hirsch, Jill Kneerim, Laura Marris, Gail Mazur, James McMichael, Anita Patterson, Orlando Patterson, Carl Phillips, Ellen Pinsky, Nicole Pinsky, Philip Schultz, Tom Sleigh, Nicole Sealey, Norman Steinberg, David Thorburn and Tomas Unger.

—R. P.

CREDITS